MISSISSIPPI MEMORIES

MISSISSIPPI MEMORIES

CLASSIC AMERICAN COOKING FROM THE HEARTLAND TO THE MISSISSIPPI BAYOU

RICK RODGERS AND THE DELTA QUEEN STEAMBOAT CO., INC.

HEARST BOOKS   NEW YORK

Photographs courtesy of the Collection of Thomas H. and Joan W. Gandy, except for the following: pages 19, 42, 43, 54, 55, 79, 89, 93 and 94, 124, 153, 173, 177, courtesy of Delta Queen Steamboat Company; page 17, courtesy of The Mark Twain Museum, Hannibal, Missouri; pages 6–7, 16, 82–83, and 117, courtesy of the Public Library of Cincinnati and Hamilton County, Rare Book/Inland Rivers Collection; pages 99, 152–153, courtesy of C. W. Stoll Collection; page 155, Greene Family Collection; page 163 (steamboat), courtesy of H. Armstrong Roberts, Inc.

It is the policy of William Morrow and Company, Inc., and its imprints and affiliates, recognizing the importance of preserving what has been written, to print the books we publish on acid-free paper, and we exert our best efforts to that end.

Library of Congress Cataloging-in-Publication Data

Rodgers, Rick, 1953–
    Mississippi memories / by Rick Rodgers and the Delta Queen Steamboat Company.
        p.   cm.
    Includes index.
    ISBN 0-688-12799-1
    1. Cookery, American.   2. Cookery—Mississippi River Region.   3. River boats—Mississippi River—History.   I. Delta Queen Steamboat Company.   II. Title.
TX715.R679   1994
641.5973—dc20
                                                                                                94-4163
                                                                                                  CIP

Printed in the United States of America

First Edition

1 2 3 4 5 6 7 8 9 10

BOOK DESIGN BY RENATO STANISIC

Acknowledgments

⚓

The writing of this cookbook was like one long Mardi Gras party. Many people—some new friends, some old pals—attended the festivities.

Diane Kniss and I met in a kitchen over ten years ago, and we have been having a good time cooking together since. Judith Dunbar Hines, who grew up on the Mississippi, shared jokes with us while we worked, and also supplied a number of recipes from her family. Friends up and down the river sent recipes from their regions, particularly Stephen Lee in Louisville and Lois Lee in Minneapolis. Patrick Charles, owner of Lucullus, New Orleans' foremost culinary antiques store, shared his insights on steamboat cuisine. The staff at the New Orleans Historical Society was the epitome of Southern graciousness and efficiency.

Two steamboat periodicals were very helpful: *The S & D Reflector* and *The Egregious Steamboat Journal*. Many of their readers were kind enough to send recollections and mementos of river travel, especially Walt Thayer and Mike Giglio, who also sent me a copy of the American Sternwheel Association's fundraiser cookbook.

Connie Fox and Patti Young of The Delta Queen Steamboat Co., Inc., have become great friends as well as colleagues since our first meeting over helpings of bread pudding almost two years ago. The entire staff and crews of the *Queens* were helpful and hospitable. Thanks also goes to Megan Newman, Bill Adler, Harriet Bell, and Susan Ginsburg.

CONTENTS

STUFFIN' GOOD:

RIVER FARE

Lounging in my deck chair, totally, perhaps overly, relaxed, I sipped my coffee at a leisurely pace as the steamboat meandered by the tree-lined riverbanks and farm fields. She was propelled by her huge paddle wheel and as she glided quietly on the slate-gray of the Mississippi, the only sound was a gentle whooshing, as soothing as a babbling fountain. The *Delta Queen* moved with the slightest rocking sensation, and my mind and body tricked themselves into believing that I was a coddled baby—I had to shake myself often to keep from falling asleep midnovel, no matter how much chicory-scented coffee I drank.

Of the twelve thousand steamboats that once plied the rivers, now only six are left, and just three that still greet overnight passengers: The Delta Queen Steamboat Co.'s *Delta Queen* and *Mississippi Queen*, and the newest addition, the *American Queen*. The grand traditions of riverboat hospitality are stylishly upheld as The Delta Queen Steamboat Co.'s passengers board in New Orleans, Memphis, St. Louis, and St. Paul/Minneapolis among other cities, and stop in towns rich in history such as Natchez, Vicksburg, Baton Rouge, and Hannibal. The *Queen*s do not just ply the Mississippi, but also the Ohio, Tennessee, Arkansas, Cumberland, and the Cajun country's Atchafalaya. Great steamboatin' cities like Louisville, Cincinnati, and Pittsburgh are also ports of call.

The golden age of riverboat passenger travel flourished from about 1870 to 1900. Once, hundreds of "floating palaces" worked America's Southern and Eastern rivers, establishing in our consciousness images of graceful, unhurried travel, and of cotton bales, hoopskirts, and mint juleps. In order to lure travelers away from their quicker arch-rivals, the railroads, the post–Civil War steamboat companies built passenger boats of unparalleled luxury, comparable to the best hotels. Of course, fine dining was a major draw. The tables were spectacularly set with the most elegant Sèvres china and Reed and Barton silver. The *J. M. White* featured an enormous silver watercooler with sterling silver mugs for its first-class passengers to refresh themselves. The Anchor Line was known for its special way of setting the table, with the silverware precariously and dramatically balanced in a decorative tower in front of each plate.

Guests were treated to sumptuous meals created from the best ingredients.

The largest boats spent about two thousand dollars a week on groceries—during a period when chickens were a dime each and a pound of butter cost less than a nickel. When Effie Ellsler, billed as "America's Greatest Actress," was a passenger on the *St. Joseph* on the Natchez-Vicksburg line in 1896, the chef made a great show in each port to obtain the absolutely finest victuals for his important guest.

Most of the time, purveying edibles was done more simply. The farmers who lived on the riverbanks were well aware of how important the boats were to their livelihood and were happy to provide the cooks with produce from their crops along the way (refrigeration was virtually nonexistent). It was not unusual to find signs stating FIRST TWO ROWS FOR RIVERBOATS. HELP YOURSELF. Some salted and pickled meats and fish were stored on board in barrels. Livestock was kept below decks and butchered as needed. The slang for useless stuff, "hogwash," refers to the offal rinsed off into the rivers.

America believed that it had to be well fed to grapple with the responsibilities of Manifest Destiny, and riverboat menus were enormous. The menu from the *Robert F. Ward*, March 12, 1853, is especially interesting considering most historians agree that the steamboats upgraded their culinary offerings only after the Civil War. This example shows that the antebellum *cartes'* fare was pretty impressive too. I have not corrected the menu's misspellings and abbreviations.

SOUP

Green Sea Turtle

FISH

Redfish, Baked, Browned Oyster Sauce   Sheepshead, Boiled
Broiled Trout Mad[iera]. Wine Sauce

BOILED

Ham   Mutton [Capers]   Corned Beef   Turkey with Oyster Sauce   Tongue
Chicken Eggs   Spiced Round of Beef

ENTREES

Knuck[le] of Veal,   Green Peas   Turkey Wings,   Celery Sauce
Crabs,   Stuffed   Pigs Head,   Tomato Sauce   Oyster Pie   Shoulder of Lamb,
Green Peas   Turtle Cutlets,   Mad[iera]. Wine Sauce
Macaroni, à la Neopolitaine

ROASTS

Beef Pork Pig Mutton Turkey Chicken Veal Duck

VEGETABLES OF THE SEASON

GAME

Saddle of Venison with Cranberry Sauce   French Duck with Currant Jelly
Black Duck Smothered in Wine Sauce   Grouse, Stuffed, with Lemon Sauce

PASTRY AND DESSERT

Orange, Coconut, Lemon, Green Apple, Mince, Cherry,
Cranberry and Gooseberry Pies   Apple, Grape and Whortleberry Tarts   Pineapple Cream
Puffs   Fruit, Citron and Tapioca Puddings   Prune, Fruit, Sponge
and Jelly Cakes   Calle Fritters   Lady Fingers   Charlotte Russe
Blanchemange   English and Coconut Cream   White Wine and Rum Jellies
Pineapple Sherbert Rose and Lemon Ice Creams

FRUIT

Oranges,   Bananas,   Figs,   Grapes,   Prunes,   Raisins,   Apples
Almonds,   Walnuts,   Pecans,   Filberts

Sauternes and Claret Wines

Coffee

In first-class, breakfast was served from seven to ten in the morning, with the largest meal, dinner, at two in the afternoon. Tea, or supper, was a light repast at six-thirty. On most boats, these mealtimes were unshakable. Meals were served in the main cabin, as most steamboats simply did not have enough room for separate dining areas. Dining accoutrements were stored away between meals to leave the cabin available for socializing, musicales, and card games.

The boats offered impeccable service by a white-jacketed black staff, which evidence shows was sometimes too attentive. An 1886 advertisement for a steamboat company announced that it had established a new policy to avoid guests being constantly interrupted by overzealous waiters. Henceforth, it said, waiters "would stand off at a reasonable distance from the table and when their presence is desired, the one wishing it gives a slight tap to the bell."

Unfortunately, the dining conditions were not as elegant in second class, where the steerage passengers, or cargo rustlers, were simply served the leftovers from the wealthier guests' meals. The remains were unceremoniously dumped in three pans—one for meat and potatoes, one for bread, and one for desserts—and served buffet style. Many an argument broke out over a rustler who grabbed too much meat.

As the riverboats traveled up and down the rivers, they carried more than passengers and cargo—they carried ideas, music, and recipes. Before riverboat travel, American food was highly localized, the Scandinavian and German cooks of the north knowing little about the spicy foods of the bayou hundreds of miles away. It doesn't seem that any particular dishes were invented on board

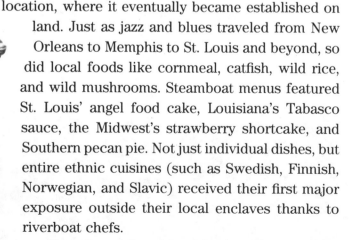

steamboats, but a dish that a cook would taste in one port would end up on the boat menu and travel to another location, where it eventually became established on land. Just as jazz and blues traveled from New Orleans to Memphis to St. Louis and beyond, so did local foods like cornmeal, catfish, wild rice, and wild mushrooms. Steamboat menus featured St. Louis' angel food cake, Louisiana's Tabasco sauce, the Midwest's strawberry shortcake, and Southern pecan pie. Not just individual dishes, but entire ethnic cuisines (such as Swedish, Finnish, Norwegian, and Slavic) received their first major exposure outside their local enclaves thanks to riverboat chefs.

French and Spanish cuisines combined to influence the cooking of the most important river city, New Orleans. France was the first major

player in the history of New Orleans. French explorers often ventured down from Canada searching for the elusive Northwest Passage and, failing, began a lucrative fur trade with the Native Americans. In 1673, Marquette and Jolliet explored the Mississippi as far as the mouth of the Arkansas River. Robert de La Salle and his expedition reached the Gulf of Mexico in 1682 and perfunctorily claimed for his country all land drained by the river and its tributaries. A period of sporadic French settlement started at present-day Natchez with the first permanent white colony on the Mississippi established in 1716, although Vicksburg also lays claim to this distinction.

Two years later, New Orleans was founded to help ship the river's bounty to the European markets. New Orleans remained French territory until 1762, when it was ceded to Spain as one of the spoils of a political dispute. Wealthy Spaniards then arrived, and their tomatoes and garlic were added to the established French style of cooking. A few years later, French aristocrats fleeing the French Revolution came to New Orleans, and brought their chefs with them. The intermarried race of Louisianans became known as Creole (from the Spanish *Criollo* for "native"), and its food reflected its blue-blooded origins, with an emphasis on fine sauces and refined cooking techniques.

Another group of French settlers came to the Louisiana bayou in the 1760s, creating another kind of cuisine there. Catholic French Canadians living in Acadia (now Nova Scotia) were deported by the British, who cruelly separated the men from the women and children. After ten years of wandering, some of the survivors were finally reunited in New Orleans, where they were welcomed by the Catholic Creoles. As the Acadians (or "Cajuns" as the Creoles mispronounced them) were used to a rugged life in Canada, they felt at home facing the challenges of life in the bayou. Cajun food is reminiscent of the lusty ragouts of their ancestors, enlived by the additions of local game, such as duck, and crawfish.

Of all the river cuisines, the heady Louisiana-style cooking is the best known, with just about every American city today boasting an ersatz Cajun/Creole restaurant. The food at these restaurants often suffers from being adapted, sometimes being quite a pale version of the vibrant, exciting food enjoyed by diners in New Orleans restaurants. In some cuisines, dishes are described nostalgically as things that Grandma made once upon a time, but, alas, just don't seem to get cooked much anymore. Louisianans will have none of that! On practically every street corner (and not just in the touristy French Quarter), real New Orleans fare, the same as in times gone by, can be detected by the wonderful aromas wafting out through a restaurant door or the open window of a house. Red beans and rice, gumbo, jambalaya, fried shrimp with remoulade sauce, po' boy sandwiches (fried shellfish on a French roll), oysters Rockefeller, beignets (doughnutlike fritters), calas (hot rice cakes), boiled crawfish—these dishes are found on menus everywhere, washed down with plenty of Abita beer or bourbon.

Louisiana cuisine has tended to overshadow the other fine river cooking traditions, and not because these cuisines are any less delicious. While New Orleans food is Mediterranean-influenced, the tastes of northern Europe dominate the menus farther north. German and Scandinavian immigrants began to arrive in the upper-river regions in the 1830s, attracted by reports that there was land available for the taking, which included forests, lakes, and long cold winters like in their homelands. The soil was perfect for the foods they loved—potatoes, rutabagas, carrots, cabbage, rye, barley, and dried beans—and the lakes teemed with freshwater fish for cooking, smoking, or pickling in vinegar. Many of these pioneers were refugees from religious persecution and brought a reverent dedication to their hard work in the fields, making the region famous for its produce and livestock. Others, such as the British and Slavs, came to work in Minnesota's iron foundries and mills.

This book is a sampler of my favorite recipes gathered from river cooks from Minneapolis to New Orleans, from Louisville to Pittsburgh. Space constraints meant the list had to be selective, for a full listing of the region's specialties would easily require five or six books. Some of the recipes are verbatim from my sources and others are interpretations or reworkings of classic dishes. Occasionally, with an eye to current healthy cooking, I have developed reduced-fat versions, but only in recipes where the changes aren't jarring. A book on classic American cooking is not the place to look for low-fat desserts, for example.

At the end of many recipes you will find a few words of advice, guidance, or caution that are not in the instructions—a *lagniappe*. Here's the description of a lagniappe by the best-known chronicler of river life, Mark Twain:

> "We picked up one excellent word—a word worth traveling to New Orleans to get; a nice, limber, expressive, handy word—'lagniappe.' They pronounce it lanny-*yap*. It is Spanish—so they said. We discovered it at the head of a column of odds and ends in the *Picayune* the first day; heard twenty people use it the second; inquired what it meant the third; adopted it and got facility in swinging it the fourth. It is the equivalent of the thirteenth roll in a 'baker's dozen.' It is sometimes thrown in, gratis, for good measure. When a child or servant buys something in a shop—or even the mayor or governor, for aught I know—he finished the operation by saying: 'Give me something for lagniappe.' The shopman always responds; gives the child a bit of licorice-root, gives the servant a cheap cigar or a spool of thread, gives the governor—I don't know what he gives the governor; support, likely."

There's no better way to start a trip on the Mississippi than with the words of Mark Twain, so let's cast off!

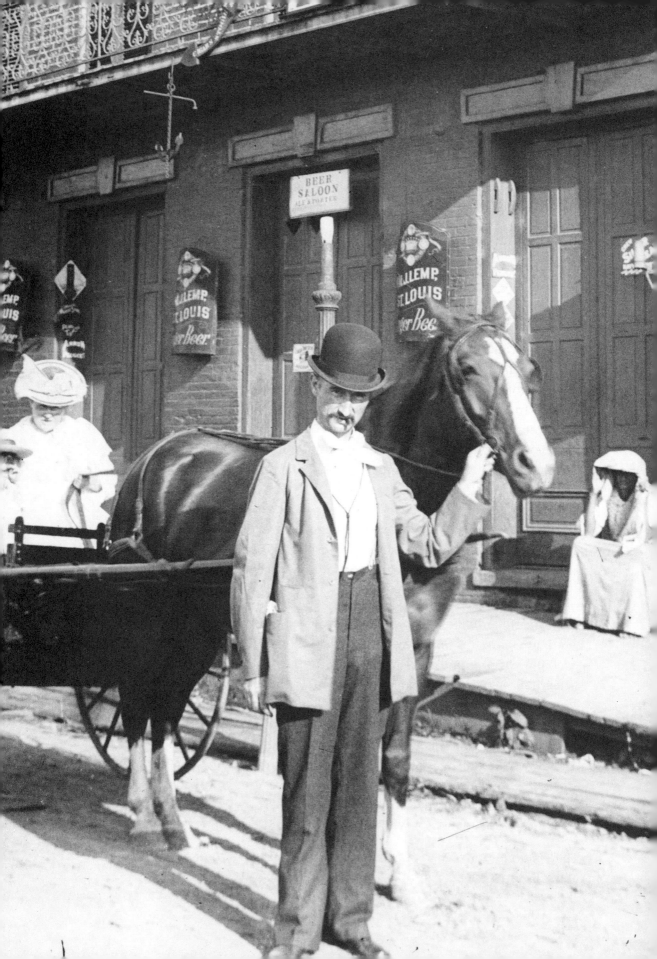

PUSHING OFF: APPETIZERS, SOUPS,

HORS D'OEUVRES, AND BEVERAGES

Creole Shellfish Spread
with Benne Wafers

⚓

Here's a zesty appetizer sure to be a crowd pleaser that is reminiscent of a shrimp cocktail on a cracker. If you have access to crayfish tails, use them for authentic Creole flavor, but cooked shrimp and crab are admirable stand-ins. Locals would use Creole cream cheese, a tart product unavailable outside of the area (and darned hard to find in New Orleans), but its flavor is approximated by the cream cheese and sour cream mixture in the recipe. Sesame crackers are popular throughout the South, and are often called by their old Africa-originated name, "benne" wafers.

Makes 6 to 8 servings

1 8-ounce package cream cheese, at room temperature
2 tablespoons sour cream
1 cup bottled chili sauce
1 celery rib, finely chopped
1 scallion, finely chopped
1 tablespoon chopped fresh parsley
1 tablespoon fresh lemon juice
1 tablespoon bottled horseradish
Hot pepper sauce to taste
Lettuce leaves
2 cups (about 8 ounces) cooked crawfish tails, deveined chopped shrimp, or crabmeat
Sesame crackers, for serving

1. In a medium bowl, combine the softened cream cheese and sour cream with a wooden spoon. Line a 1½-cup bowl or mold with plastic wrap. Fill the bowl with the cream cheese mixture, cover, and refrigerate for at least 4 hours, until chilled.

2. In a medium bowl, combine the chili sauce, celery, scallion, parsley, lemon juice, horseradish, and hot pepper sauce. Cover and chill for at least 1 hour, or overnight.

3. Arrange the lettuce leaves in a spoke pattern on a round serving platter. Invert the cream cheese mixture onto the center of the platter, removing the plastic wrap. Stir the crawfish tails into the chili sauce mixture. Pour over the cheese mold and serve immediately with sesame crackers.

The classic 1927 musical play, Show Boat, by Jerome Kern and Oscar Hammerstein II, based on Edna Ferber's novel, established the image of river life in American culture through three film versions and countless stage productions. The latest Broadway version, directed by Harold Prince, is scheduled to open in 1994. In most stagings, the showboat itself is an elaborate affair, based more on the passenger boat "palaces" than on the true authentic designs. Real showboats were never ornate paddle wheelers, but simple barges that were pushed along the river by larger steamboats.

Oven Bobby-Cued Shrimp

⚓

This is my own adaptation of New Orleans "barbecued shrimp." Unlike the Worcestershire and butter sauce found in restaurants, my version has a spicy to-mato-based marinade. (Be sure to allow plenty of time for the shrimp to mari-nate—at least four hours.) Have extra bowls handy for the shells and present plenty of napkins for this finger-lickin'-good dish! It's quite an icebreaker, and you will find it fun, messy, and absolutely delicious, in equally enjoyable measures.

Makes 6 servings as an appetizer

8 tablespoons (1 stick) unsalted butter
1 small onion, chopped
3 garlic cloves, minced
1 cup olive oil
¾ cup tomato purée
2 tablespoons Worcestershire sauce
1 tablespoon Bayou Seasoning (page 46)

1 teaspoon dried oregano
1 teaspoon dried rosemary
½ teaspoon crushed red pepper flakes
¼ teaspoon salt
1 lemon, halved
2 pounds medium shrimp, unshelled
Crusty Italian or French bread, for dipping

1. In a medium skillet, melt the butter over medium-low heat. Add the onion and garlic and cook until softened but not browned, about 3 minutes.

2. Add the olive oil, tomato purée, Worcestershire sauce, Bayou Seasoning, oregano, rosemary, red pepper, and salt. Squeeze the juice from the lemon and add the juice with the lemon halves to the sauce. Bring the sauce to a simmer and simmer over low heat, stirring often, for 10 minutes.

3. Transfer the sauce to a 13 × 9-inch glass baking dish and cool completely. Stir in the shrimp, cover, and refrigerate at least 4 hours, or overnight.

4. Preheat the oven to 350°F. Bake the shrimp, stirring often, until they are pink and firm, about 20 minutes. With a slotted spoon, transfer the shrimp to soup bowls. Transfer the sauce, discarding the lemon halves, to a blender and purée until smooth, about 1 minute. Pour the hot sauce evenly over the shrimp and serve immediately with the crusty bread for dipping. (The sauce will sep-arate upon standing, but you will be eating this dish so fast, you won't notice.)

Mississippi River Fish, Corn, and Bacon Chowder

⚓

Just about any fish would be happy to be found swimming in this indulgent, rich, and creamy soup. I've used that Southern star of the river's fishnet—catfish. Recently, many aquaculture farms have been established in the South, making catfish available all over the country. The farm-raised variety has a milder and less muddy taste, which has definitely increased its popularity. Up north, whitefish, perch, or trout (or even smoked fish) may be used.

Makes 6 to 8 servings

6 strips of bacon, cut into 1-inch-wide pieces
1 medium onion, chopped
2 scallions, chopped
2 celery ribs, chopped into 1/4-inch-thick slices
1 sweet red bell pepper, seeded, stemmed, and chopped into 1/2-inch pieces
1 garlic clove, minced
1/3 cup all-purpose flour
1 tablespoon Bayou Seasoning (page 46)

2 1/2 cups bottled clam juice
2 1/2 cups water
2 medium boiling potatoes, unpeeled, scrubbed, and cut into 3/4-inch cubes
1 pound catfish, cut into 1-inch chunks
1 cup heavy cream
1 cup fresh or defrosted frozen corn kernels
1/2 teaspoon salt or to taste
1/4 teaspoon hot pepper sauce or to taste
Chopped fresh chives or parsley, for garnish

1. In a large soup pot, cook the bacon over medium heat, turning occasionally, until crisp, about 5 minutes. Using a slotted spoon, transfer the bacon to paper towels to drain, then crumble and set aside. Pour off all but 2 tablespoons of the fat in the pot.

2. In the same pot, cook the onion, scallion, celery, red bell pepper, and garlic, covered, stirring often, until softened, about 5 minutes. Add the flour and Bayou Seasoning and stir constantly until the flour is absorbed, about 1 minute.

3. Add the clam juice and water and bring to a simmer, scraping up the flavorful bits from the bottom of the pot with a wooden spoon. Stir in the potatoes and bring to a simmer. Reduce the heat to low and simmer, partially covered, until the potatoes are tender, about 30 minutes. (The soup can be prepared up to this point 1 day ahead of serving. Cool, refrigerate, then return to a simmer over low heat before proceeding.)

4. Stir in the catfish, heavy cream, and corn and cook until the fish is just firm and opaque, about 5 minutes. Season to taste with salt and hot pepper sauce. Serve, sprinkling each serving with the crumbled bacon and chopped chives.

Lagniappe: If you are a "from scratch" cook, this chowder is even better with 5 cups homemade fish stock instead of the 2½ cups each bottled clam juice and water.

The strongest earthquake ever to strike North America occurred on December 11, 1811 near New Madrid (pronounced MAD-rid), Missouri. The course of the Mississippi changed and the river actually ran backward. Although the area was only sparsely populated by white settlers, Congress passed an act that allowed them to resettle on other tracts of public land, making this one of the first acts of social welfare by the government. The sight was witnessed by the passengers on the New Orleans's maiden voyage, the first steamboat to make the trip from Pittsburgh to Natchez.

CHARLES REBSTOCK

Steamboats let their presence be known with billows of steam and the shrill cry of their whistles as they puffed along the river. Each riverboat was equipped with a whistle, like the three-tube version atop the Charles Rebstock, whose sound was that boat's unique signature. Sometimes eerie, sometimes melodious, and sometimes downright sour, the whistles were audible long before the boat appeared around the bend.

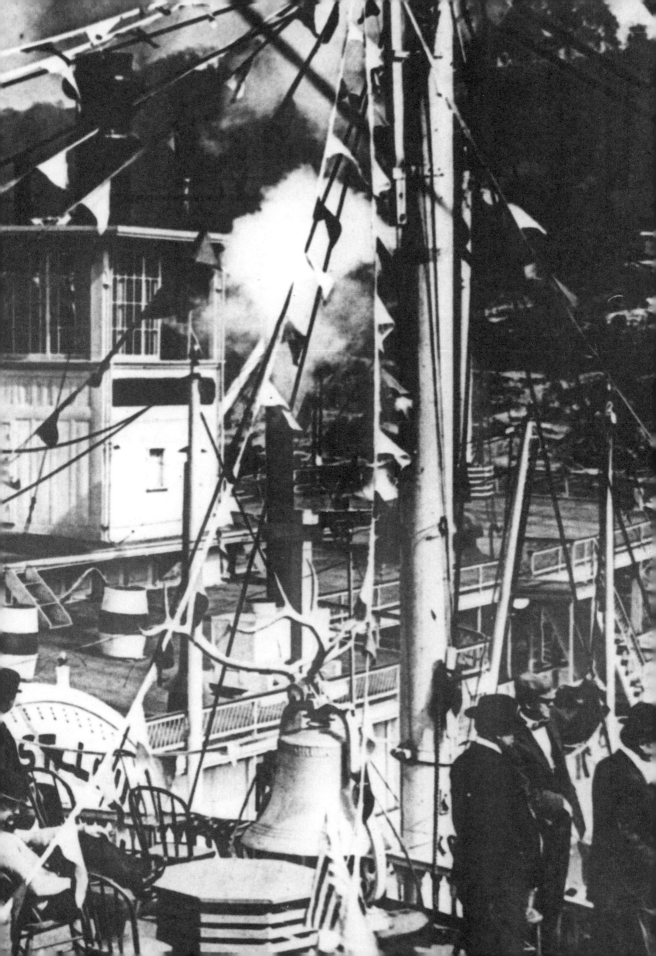

Oysters Rockefeller Bisque

⚓

Oysters Rockefeller, created by New Orleans's Antoine's Restaurant, are bi-valves cloaked and baked in a sauce so rich and currency-green that it was named for the era's wealthiest man, John D. Rockefeller. I've taken the hallmark ingredients from Antoine's recipe, and have combined them with a few others for an elegant, yet easy to make soup.

Makes 6 servings

1 tablespoon unsalted butter

¼ cup minced shallots or scallion

2 celery ribs, finely chopped

2 cups bottled clam juice

2 cups water

1 10-ounce package frozen chopped spinach, defrosted and squeezed dry

¼ cup chopped fresh parsley

½ teaspoon dried tarragon

1 tablespoon cornstarch

2 tablespoons water

1 tablespoon anise-flavored liqueur, such as Pernod

1 cup evaporated skimmed milk or half-and-half

18 shucked oysters, including the oyster juices

½ teaspoon salt or to taste

½ teaspoon hot pepper sauce or to taste

1. In a large soup pot, melt the butter over low heat. Add the shallots and celery. Cook, covered, until softened, about 5 minutes. Stir in the clam juice, water, spinach, parsley, and tarragon and bring to a simmer over medium-high heat. Reduce the heat to low and simmer for 30 minutes. (The soup can be prepared up to this point 1 day ahead of serving. Cool, refrigerate, then return to a simmer over low heat before proceeding.)

2. In a small bowl, sprinkle the cornstarch over the water and liqueur and stir to dissolve. Add the liqueur mixture and the evaporated skim milk to the soup pot and bring just to the simmer, stirring often.

3. Add the oysters with their liquid and cook until oysters are just firm and plump, about 3 minutes. Season to taste with salt and hot pepper sauce. Serve immediately.

Lagniappe: Substitute 4 cups homemade fish stock for the 2 cups each bottled clam juice and water.

B*iloxi, Mississippi, was once such an important oyster-fishing center that its streets were paved with oyster shells.*

Lean Turkey Gumbo

⚓

Gumbo is a stick-to-your-ribs soup so chunky that I have often been served bowls of it that could support a standing spoon. The soup's thickness is achieved by using a cooked flour and oil roux in tandem with either slices of okra or a spoonful of filé (ground sassafras) powder. The okra and filé powder give gumbo its characteristic gelatinous texture, though a Cajun cook usually uses just one or the other, never both in the same pot. Roux is traditionally cooked with equal parts of flour and oil, but, inspired by Paul Prudhomme's new, trimmed-down recipes, lately I have been toasting the flour alone in a skillet, and it works beautifully. Made with lower-fat turkey drumsticks and turkey kielbasa, this fashionably lean version is attractive indeed. Gumbo can be either a substantial first course or a light lunch or supper dish.

Makes 8 to 10 servings

½ cup all-purpose flour
Nonstick vegetable cooking
  spray
12 ounces smoked turkey
  kielbasa, cut into
  ½-inch-thick slices
1 medium onion, chopped
2 celery ribs with leaves,
  cut into ¼-inch-thick
  slices
2 medium sweet red bell
  peppers, seeded,
  stemmed, and cut into
  ½-inch pieces
4 scallions, chopped
3 garlic cloves, minced
6 cups chicken stock,
  preferably homemade, or

low-sodium canned
  chicken broth
3 turkey drumsticks (about
  2¼ pounds total)
1 28-ounce can Italian
  peeled tomatoes, drained
  and coarsely chopped
¼ cup chopped fresh
  parsley
1 tablespoon plus
  1 teaspoon Bayou
  Seasoning (page 46)
2 bay leaves
1 tablespoon filé powder
Salt to taste
Hot pepper sauce to taste
4 cups hot freshly cooked
  long-grain rice

1. Preheat a large nonstick skillet over medium heat for 2 minutes. Add the flour and stir constantly, shaking the pan often, until the flour has turned dark beige, about 5 minutes. Do not let the flour scorch. Immediately transfer the browned flour to a plate and set aside.

2. Spray the same skillet lightly with nonstick vegetable spray. Add the kielbasa slices, onion, celery, red bell pepper, scallion, and garlic. Cover and cook over medium heat for 5 minutes. Uncover and cook, stirring occasionally, until the vegetables are lightly browned, about 6 additional minutes. Transfer to a large soup pot.

3. Stir in the reserved browned flour. Gradually stir in the chicken stock. Add the drumsticks and bring to a simmer, skimming off any foam that rises to the surface. Stir in the tomatoes, parsley, Bayou Seasoning, and bay leaves. Simmer, partially covered, until the drumsticks are tender, about 1½ hours.

4. Remove the drumsticks and let them cool slightly. Remove the meat from the bones, discarding the skin, tendons, and bones. Return the turkey to the gumbo and stir in the filé powder. Heat gently, but do not boil. Season the gumbo to taste with salt and hot pepper sauce.

5. To serve, place a large spoonful of rice in each soup bowl and ladle the gumbo over the rice.

The first steamboat to travel down the Mississippi was the New Orleans, built from a Robert Fulton design. The captain was Nicholas Roosevelt, great-uncle of Theodore. The trip took from September 1811 to January 1812. The passengers survived not only the dangerous river currents, snags, and rapids but the birth of a child on board, a fire in the front cabin, and the New Madrid earthquake.

Roast Duck and Wild Rice Soup

⚓

Wild duck is the favorite game of river huntsmen from Minneapolis to Baton Rouge. Up north, the birds nest near the wild rice paddies, and the two simmered together make a superlative soup. This is a "company's coming" soup and is best made leisurely over a two-day period. The preparation may take time, but the actual work is minimal and the results excellent. The basis for the duck stock is a roasted duck, as roasting it removes a large amount of unwanted fat, and the browned carcass adds depth of flavor.

Makes 8 to 10 servings

ROAST DUCK STOCK

1 4½- to 5-pound duck, neck and giblets reserved (not the liver)

½ teaspoon salt

¼ teaspoon freshly ground black pepper

1 cup boiling water

1 large carrot, coarsely chopped

1 large onion, coarsely chopped

1 medium celery rib, coarsely chopped

1 cup plus 2 quarts cold water, divided

4 parsley sprigs

½ teaspoon dried thyme

1 bay leaf

¼ teaspoon whole black peppercorns

DUCK AND WILD RICE SOUP

2 tablespoons unsalted butter

6 scallions, chopped

3 celery ribs, cut into ¼-inch-thick slices

2 medium carrots, cut into ½-inch cubes

8 ounces white mushrooms, thinly sliced

2 quarts Roast Duck Stock

¼ cup chopped fresh parsley

1½ teaspoons dried savory or thyme

1 teaspoon salt

¼ teaspoon freshly ground black pepper

¾ cup wild rice, well rinsed and drained

Sour cream, for garnish (optional)

1. *Make the Roast Duck Stock.* Make the stock at least 1 day ahead. Preheat the oven to 400°F. Rinse the duck, remove the excess fat from the tail cavity, and pat dry with paper towels. Sprinkle the cavity of the duck with the salt and pepper. With the upturned prongs of a serving fork, pierce the duck skin all over, being careful not to pierce the meat.

2. Place the duck on a rack in a roasting pan and slowly pour the boiling water over the top of the duck. Roast, basting often, for 45 minutes. Place the carrot, onion, celery, and duck neck and giblets in the pan and continue to roast, basting often, until the juices run clear when the thigh is pierced with a fork, about 1 hour. Set the duck aside until cool enough to handle. When the duck has cooled, remove as much meat as possible, discarding the skin and fat. Cut the meat into ½-inch cubes, cover, and refrigerate.

3. Using a slotted spoon, transfer the vegetables, neck, and giblets to a large soup pot. (The rendered duck fat in the bottom of the roasting pan can be reserved, covered and refrigerated, to use in cooking.) Place the roasting pan over two burners on top of the stove and add 1 cup cold water. Bring to a simmer, scraping up any flavorful bits from the bottom of the pan, then pour into the soup pot.

4. Add the duck carcass and wings to the soup pot and add the 2 quarts of cold water. Bring to a simmer over medium heat, skimming off and discarding any foam that rises to the surface. Add the parsley, thyme, bay leaf, and peppercorns. Reduce the heat to low and simmer for 2 hours. Strain the broth and let cool to room temperature. Refrigerate at least 4 hours or overnight, until well chilled. Lift off and discard the hard fat on top of the stock. (The stock can be prepared up to 3 days ahead, covered and refrigerated.)

5. *Make the Soup.* In a large pot over medium-low heat, cook the butter, scallion, celery, carrot, and mushrooms, covered, until the vegetables have softened, about 5 minutes. Add the duck stock, parsley, savory, salt, and pepper and bring to a simmer. Add the wild rice and simmer over low heat, partially covered, until the rice is tender, about 1 hour to 1 hour and 15 minutes. Add the duck meat cubes and heat through, about 5 minutes. Serve immediately, topping each serving with a dollop of sour cream if desired.

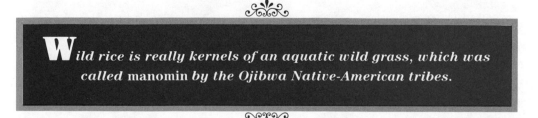

Wild rice is really kernels of an aquatic wild grass, which was called manomin by the Ojibwa Native-American tribes.

The calliope, which shrilly announces the arrival of a steamboat, is one of the three unique American musical instruments, along with the tuba and the banjo. It was invented in 1855 by a church musician who wanted to improve upon the standard organ. His congregation rebelled at his calliope's somewhat unusual musical sound,

and his brother took it off his hands and installed it as a whistle on his steamboat which ran the Hudson River. P. T. Barnum heard a calliope on a boat on the Ohio River in 1875 and transferred it to the circus, realizing the advertising benefits of a whistle that could be heard for five miles.

A Big Batch of Ramos Fizzes

⚓

According to bartending legend, this creamy, heady concoction was invented around 1888 by Henry Ramos at his New Orleans watering hole, the Imperial Cabinet (or Cabaret). Some sources attribute the drink to a Meyer's Restaurant, but the Fairmont (once the Roosevelt) Hotel nows hold the trademark Ramos Gin Fizz. Whatever its provenance, any Sunday brunch is made all the more festive when fizzes are served. Instead of a recipe for a single drink, I offer my time-tested version, which I have made by the blenderful for years. For a Golden Fizz, use whole eggs or liquid egg substitute. If you have a hard time finding orange blossom water, substitute 2 tablespoons frozen orange juice concentrate.

Makes 4 servings

1 cup gin	4 large ice cubes
½ cup half-and-half	4 egg whites or 2 large eggs
½ cup lime juice	or ½ cup liquid egg
¼ cup sugar	substitute
1½ teaspoons orange blossom water	Approximately ½ cup chilled club soda

1. In a blender, combine the gin, half-and-half, lime juice, sugar, orange blossom water, ice cubes, and egg whites. Blend on high until well mixed.

2. Pour into individual serving glasses and top off each glass with approximately 2 tablespoons club soda to provide the "fizz." Serve immediately.

Lagniappe: Orange blossom water is available at specialty food stores and by mail order from The Baker's Catalogue, RR 2, P.O. Box 56, Norwich, VT 05055 (1-800-827-6836). It is also delicious used as a flavoring for pound cakes.

Toasted Ravioli with Tomato Gravy Dip

⚓

Many St. Louis restaurants, from fast-food joints to fine Italian trattorias, serve these fun-to-eat morsels. Deep-fried, cheese-filled ravioli, dipped in a fragrant tomato sauce, are a special treat that are even better when rinsed down with cold beer.

Makes 6 to 8 servings as an appetizer

TOMATO GRAVY
1 tablespoon olive oil
1 medium onion, finely chopped
1 garlic clove, minced
¾ cup beef stock
1 cup tomato purée
½ cup red wine
¼ cup tomato paste
¼ cup minced fresh parsley

1 teaspoon dried basil
1 teaspoon dried oregano
¼ teaspoon crushed red pepper flakes

TOASTED RAVIOLI
Vegetable oil for deep-frying
½ cup milk
2 large eggs
¾ cup fresh fine bread crumbs
24 1½-inch-square cheese-filled ravioli (about ½ pound)

1. In a medium saucepan over low heat, heat the olive oil and cook the onion and garlic until softened, stirring often, about 5 minutes. Add the beef stock, tomato purée, red wine, tomato paste, parsley, basil, oregano, and crushed red pepper and simmer, uncovered, for 45 minutes.

2. Preheat the oven to 200°F. In a large saucepan, heat enough oil to reach 2 inches up the sides of the pan until it is very hot but not smoking (375°F on a deep-frying thermometer). (An electric deep fryer works perfectly for this.) Be sure the oil has reached the right temperature before preparing the ravioli.

3. In a shallow bowl, beat together the milk and eggs. Place the bread crumbs in another shallow bowl. One by one, drop the ravioli into the egg and milk mixture, then into the bread crumbs to coat.

4. In batches without crowding, drop the ravioli into the hot oil. Cook until golden brown, about 3 minutes. Using a slotted spoon, transfer them to a paper towel-lined baking sheet to drain. Keep the fried ravioli warm in the oven while cooking the rest. Serve warm, not piping hot, with warmed tomato gravy for dipping.

Frankfurters (named for the city in Germany) were popularized in St. Louis by a German immigrant named Antoine Feuchwanger, who, in the 1880s, took his country's wienerwursts and put them in a bun. They were a hit at the St. Louis World's Fair in 1904. By 1906, the term hot dog *was in use. It seems to have been coined by a Hearst syndication cartoonist, T. A. Dorgan, who drew a dachshund with a sausage for a body.*

Savory Corn Fritters

⚓

This recipe, which I served for many years as a cocktail snack at parties I catered, is jazzed up with some spices, scallions, and garlic.

Makes 2 dozen

Vegetable oil for deep-frying
1½ cups all-purpose flour
¾ teaspoon baking soda
¾ teaspoon salt
¼ teaspoon cayenne pepper
1½ cups fresh or defrosted frozen corn kernels

1 large egg, beaten
2 scallions, minced
1 garlic clove, minced
Approximately 1 cup buttermilk or 1 cup milk mixed with 1 tablespoon cider vinegar
½ cup honey, for dipping

1. Preheat the oven to 200°F. In a large saucepan, heat enough oil to reach 2 inches up the sides of the pan until it is very hot but not smoking (375°F on a deep-frying thermometer). (An electric deep fryer is perfect for this.) Be sure the oil has reached the right temperature before making the batter.

2. In a medium bowl, sift the flour, baking soda, salt, and cayenne pepper. Stir in the corn, egg, scallion, and garlic until moistened. Stir in just enough buttermilk to make a stiff batter. Do not overmix.

3. In batches without crowding, drop the batter by scant tablespoons into the hot oil. Cook until golden brown, about 3 minutes. Using a slotted spoon, transfer the fritters to a paper towel-lined baking sheet to drain. Keep the fritters warm in the oven while frying the rest of the batter.

4. Meanwhile, in a small saucepan, heat the honey over low heat until warmed. Pour it into a small bowl. Serve the warm fritters with the honey for dipping.

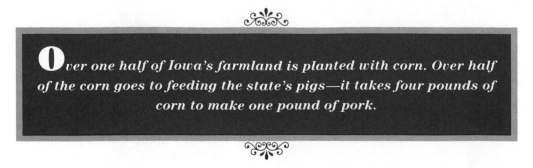

Over one half of Iowa's farmland is planted with corn. Over half of the corn goes to feeding the state's pigs—it takes four pounds of corn to make one pound of pork.

Lemon Julepade

⚓

Homemade lemonade evokes many pleasant memories of summers past. This refreshing libation is a happy marriage between a benign lemonade and "kick in the pants" mint julep. The word "julep" comes from the Persian word for rose water, *gulāb*, which is also used to make a sweet, potent drink. Serve pitchers of this mint-infused lemonade with a bottle of your favorite bourbon on the side so guests can spike their own drinks as they prefer.

Makes about 3 quarts, 10 to 12 servings

2 cups fresh lemon juice,
**   including the seeds**
1½ cups sugar
12 large mint sprigs

2 quarts ice-cold water
Approximately 1½ cups
**   bourbon**

1. In a blender, blend the lemon juice, lemon seeds, and sugar until the sugar is dissolved. Strain into a bowl to remove seeds. Divide the strained mixture and the mint sprigs between two large pitchers. Stir 1 quart of water into each pitcher. Cover and refrigerate until well chilled, at least 2 hours. (The lemonade can be prepared up to 1 day ahead, covered and refrigerated.)

2. Just before serving, pour the lemonade into tall glasses over ice, allowing each guest to add bourbon to taste.

Lagniappe: Blending the lemon seeds gives extra flavor as the lemon oil is released into the juice.

> "**N**ever insult a decent woman, never bring a horse in the house, and never crush the mint in a julep."
> *Frances Parkinson Keyes*

Spicy Fried Chicken with Buttermilk Gravy

⚓

No two cooks prepare southern fried chicken in precisely the same way. Some insist on lard or bacon fat for the proper flavor, many add a tangy note by marinating the bird in buttermilk. My method has a dash of buttermilk in the gravy and uses a modern frying-baking method which allows you to make enough for a large family dinner without using two skillets and quarts of oil.

Makes 6 to 8 servings

3 cups buttermilk, divided	2 cups all-purpose flour
2 garlic cloves, crushed through a press	¼ cup Bayou Seasoning (page 46)
1 teaspoon hot pepper sauce	1½ teaspoons salt
2 3½-pound chickens, each cut into 8 pieces	1½ cups milk
	Salt to taste
2 cups vegetable oil	Pepper to taste
	Hot pepper sauce to taste

1. In a large bowl, combine 2 cups of the buttermilk, garlic, and hot pepper sauce. Add the chicken and toss well to combine. Cover with plastic wrap and refrigerate at least 4 hours, or overnight.

2. Preheat the oven to 400°F. In a large heavy skillet, preferably black cast iron, heat the oil over medium-high heat until very hot but not smoking. In a large paper bag, combine the flour, Bayou Seasoning, and salt. Remove one third of the chicken pieces from the marinade, shaking off any excess marinade. Place the chicken pieces in the bag and shake to coat. Shake off the excess flour and place them in the skillet. Cook, turning once, until browned, about 10 minutes. (Adjust the heat so the oil stays hot but not smoking.) Transfer the cooked chicken to a large baking sheet. In two batches, repeat the browning procedure with the remaining chicken and transfer to the baking sheet. Discard the marinade, but reserve ¼ cup of the seasoned flour and leave 3 tablespoons of the oil in the skillet.

3. Bake the chicken just until it shows no sign of pink when pierced at the bone with the tip of a sharp knife, 20 to 25 minutes. Transfer to a baking sheet lined with a brown paper bag or paper towels to drain while making the gravy.

4. Return the skillet with the 3 tablespoons of oil to the stove and heat over medium-low heat. Whisk in the ¼ cup of reserved flour and let bubble gently for 2 minutes. Whisk in the milk, bring to a simmer, and cook until thickened, about 3 minutes. Whisk in the 1 cup buttermilk and cook until just heated through; do not boil. Season to taste with additional salt, pepper, and hot pepper sauce.

5. Transfer the chicken to a serving platter and serve immediately with the gravy in a warmed sauceboat.

Hot and crispy southern fried chicken was not always the year-round treat we enjoy today. Before modern breeding methods were developed in the 1920s (including controlling the temperature and light in the chicken houses to simulate desirable husbandry conditions), hens would sit on their eggs only during the warm months, so fried chicken was a seasonal dish. Huge pans of frying chicken could be found along the riverbanks to provision the kitchens of the riverbanks. (The first fast-food chicken stands?)

Skinny Cajun Chicken Loaf

⚓

Here's an updated meat loaf with an old-fashioned spirit and a new-fashioned healthy profile. The secret is the homemade Bayou Seasoning, a heady mixture of herbs and spices. This mélange can be found packaged in different proprietary blends labeled "Creole seasoning" in supermarkets all over the Mississippi delta region, but I much prefer to mix up my own in smaller, fresher, and salt-free batches. I use it as a seasoning in many of the recipes in this book, so you may want to make a double batch to store in a jar in the cupboard.

Makes 4 to 6 servings

BAYOU SEASONING
2 tablespoons paprika, preferably hot Hungarian
1 teaspoon dried basil
1 teaspoon dried thyme
½ teaspoon freshly ground black pepper
½ teaspoon garlic powder
½ teaspoon onion powder
¼ teaspoon ground hot red (cayenne) pepper, or more to taste

Nonstick vegetable cooking spray
1 medium onion, chopped

1 medium green bell pepper, seeded, stemmed, and chopped into ¼-inch pieces
1 celery rib, chopped into ¼-inch pieces
1 15-ounce can tomatoes in juice, drained and chopped
2 garlic cloves, minced
2 teaspoons Bayou Seasoning
1¼ teaspoons salt
1½ pounds ground chicken or turkey
½ cup dried bread crumbs
2 large egg whites
2 tablespoons tomato paste

1. *Make the Bayou Seasoning.* In a small bowl, combine all the ingredients and stir well. Makes about ¼ cup.

2. To make the chicken loaf, preheat the oven to 375°F. Lightly spray an 8½ × 4½ × 2½-inch loaf pan.

3. Spray a nonstick skillet with vegetable spray and place it over medium-high heat. Add the onion, green bell pepper, and celery and cook, stirring occasionally, until lightly browned, about 5 minutes. Add the tomatoes and garlic and cook, stirring often, until the juices evaporate, about 4 minutes. Stir in the Bayou Seasoning and salt. Transfer to a large bowl and cool slightly. Add the chicken, bread crumbs, and egg whites and use your hands to mix well. (Wash your hands well afterward with soap and water.)

4. Transfer to the prepared pan. Bake for 45 minutes. Spread the tomato paste evenly over the top of the loaf. Continue baking until the loaf is cooked through (a meat thermometer inserted in the center of the loaf should read 160°F), about 15 more minutes. Cool for 5 minutes before serving.

Roast Turkey with Bourbon Gravy

⚓

After roasting literally hundreds of turkeys in my career, I have three important tips—use a fresh turkey (not frozen or self-basting); stuff the bird with seasoning vegetables and bake the dressing (perhaps the Crab and Sausage Dressing on page 140) on the side; and make up a nice big batch of homemade turkey stock for the best gravy (preferably the day before roasting the turkey to free the stove burners for other goodies). My special "foil brassiere" method protects the turkey breast from drying out. If you prefer, leave out the bourbon or substitute apple cider.

Makes 15 to 20 servings

1 18-pound fresh tom turkey, neck, giblets, and gizzard removed

TURKEY STOCK
1 tablespoon vegetable oil
Neck, giblets, and gizzard from the turkey (not the liver)
1 medium onion, coarsely chopped
1 medium carrot, coarsely chopped
1 medium celery rib with leaves, coarsely chopped
4 cups chicken stock, preferably homemade, or low-sodium canned chicken broth
4 cups water
6 parsley sprigs
1 bay leaf
⅛ teaspoon peppercorns

VEGETABLE STUFFING
1 medium onion, coarsley chopped
1 medium carrot, coarsely chopped
1 medium celery rib with leaves, coarsely chopped
2 garlic cloves, minced
1 tablespoon Bayou Seasoning (page 46)
1 teaspoon salt

12 tablespoons (1½ sticks) unsalted butter, softened
1 tablespoon Bayou Seasoning (page 46)
1 teaspoon salt
½ cup all-purpose flour
6 cups Turkey Stock
3 tablespoons bourbon
Salt to taste
Pepper to taste

continued

1. The day before roasting, rinse the turkey well, inside and out, with cold running water. Pat dry with paper towels. Place the turkey on a rack in a large roasting pan and refrigerate, uncovered, until ready to roast. (The air-dried skin will roast up particularly crisp.)

2. *Make the Stock.* In a large saucepan, heat the oil over medium-high heat. Add the chopped turkey neck, giblets, and gizzard and cook, turning often, until browned, about 10 minutes. Add the onion, carrot, and celery and cook, covered, until the vegetables are softened, about 5 minutes. Stir in the chicken stock and water. Bring to a simmer, skimming off any foam that rises to the surface. Add the parsley, bay leaf, and peppercorns. Reduce the heat to low and simmer for 4 hours. Strain the stock, discarding the solids. Add additional water to the stock if necessary to make 6 cups liquid. Cool completely, then cover with plastic wrap and refrigerate overnight. Lift off and discard any hardened fat on the surface of the stock before proceeding.

3. *Make the Stuffing.* In a medium bowl, combine all the stuffing ingredients. Stuff the neck cavity with some of the vegetable mixture; fold the neck skin over and skewer it to the back skin. Place the remaining vegetable mixture in the body cavity and rub the cavity well with it. Using kitchen string, tie the wings close to the body and tie the drumsticks together. Rub the turkey all over with 4 tablespoons of the softened butter, then sprinkle with 1 tablespoon Bayou Seasoning and 1 teaspoon salt.

4. Preheat the oven to 325°F. Place the turkey on a rack in a large flameproof roasting pan. Tightly cover the breast area with aluminum foil. Pour 2 cups of the turkey stock in the bottom of the pan. Bake, uncovered, basting all over every 30 minutes with the juices on the bottom of the pan (lift up the foil to reach the breast area), until a meat thermometer inserted in the meaty part of the thigh (but not touching a bone) reads 180°F, about 5 hours and 40 minutes. If anytime during roasting the drippings on the bottom of the pan threaten to burn, add 1 cup water. Remove the foil during the last hour of baking to allow the skin to brown. Transfer the turkey to a large serving platter and let it stand for at least 20 minutes before carving. (If loosely covered with foil and draped with a clean towel, the turkey will stay warm for about 1 hour, leaving the oven free to bake dressing or other side dishes.)

5. *Make the Gravy.* While the turkey is standing, pour the drippings from the roasting pan into a glass bowl or measuring cup. Let stand for 5 minutes, then skim off and discard the clear yellow fat that rises to the top. Add the drippings to the remaining 4 cups turkey stock for the gravy.

6. Place the roasting pan over two burners. Add the remaining 8 tablespoons of butter and melt over medium-low heat. Add the flour and whisk constantly for 2 minutes. Whisk in the turkey stock and bring to a simmer. Cook until thickened to desired consistency, about 5 minutes. Whisk in the bourbon and cook for 1 minute. Season to taste with salt and pepper. Transfer the gravy to a warmed gravy boat.

7. Carve the turkey and serve the gravy alongside. Do not serve the stuffing vegetables—they are only for seasoning.

Lagniappe: Different size birds have varying roasting times: Hen turkeys (8 to 15 pounds) take about 20 minutes per pound. The larger toms (15 pounds and up) take 15 minutes per pound. If you are stuffing the bird with bread dressing, add about 5 minutes per pound for either size bird.

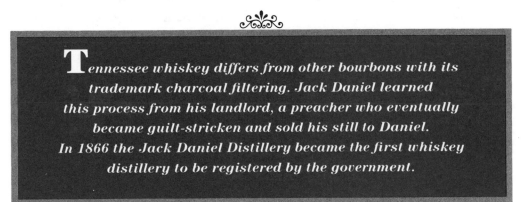

Tennessee whiskey differs from other bourbons with its trademark charcoal filtering. Jack Daniel learned this process from his landlord, a preacher who eventually became guilt-stricken and sold his still to Daniel. In 1866 the Jack Daniel Distillery became the first whiskey distillery to be registered by the government.

Eggplant and Cheddar Crisp

⚓

It seems that every church cookbook from the southern Mississippi region has a recipe for an eggplant casserole of some description, and most recipes can be a little lackluster. This is a reduced-fat version that takes the best features of the homey recipes. It is the perfect main course for a vegetarian supper or can be a rich side dish for simple roast meats.

Makes 6 to 8 servings

3 medium (1½ pounds each) eggplants, trimmed
1 tablespoon plus ¼ teaspoon salt
Nonstick vegetable cooking spray
¼ cup olive oil
3 cups Creole Tomato Sauce (page 60)
1½ cups (6 ounces) shredded reduced-fat sharp Cheddar cheese
1 cup low-fat milk
1 large egg

2 large egg whites
⅛ teaspoon freshly ground black pepper
1½ cups fresh bread crumbs, made from day-old crusty bread
1 teaspoon dried oregano
⅛ teaspoon ground red pepper
1 tablespoon unsalted butter, cut into small pieces

1. Cut the eggplants lengthwise into ½-inch-thick slices. Place them in a colander and toss with the 1 tablespoon of salt. Let them stand to draw off the bitter juices, about 45 minutes.

2. Preheat the oven to 450°F. Rinse the eggplant slices well and pat dry with paper towels. Spray two large baking sheets with nonstick vegetable spray. Arrange the eggplant slices on the baking sheets and drizzle with the olive oil. Bake, turning them once, until the eggplant is just tender and lightly browned, about 15 minutes.

3. Lower the oven temperature to 350°F. Spread about 1 cup of the Creole Tomato Sauce in the bottom of a lightly oiled 13 × 9-inch baking pan. Arrange

half of the eggplant slices in the pan, then spread with 1 cup of the remaining sauce. Sprinkle with 1 cup of the Cheddar cheese. Top with the remaining slices.

4. In a small bowl, whisk the milk, egg, egg whites, remaining ¼ teaspoon salt, and black pepper. Pour the egg mixture evenly over the eggplant, shaking the pan to allow the mixture to reach the bottom of the pan. Spread the top with the remaining 1 cup of sauce.

5. In a medium bowl, combine the remaining ½ cup Cheddar cheese, bread crumbs, oregano, and ground red pepper. Sprinkle the top of the casserole with the bread crumb mixture, then dot with the butter. Bake until crisp and bubbling and the top is golden brown, 30 to 40 minutes. Let stand about 5 minutes before serving.

The Delta Queen *was built in Stockton, California, in 1926 and operated as a ferry between San Francisco and Sacramento until 1940. My father spent summers on an island in the Sacramento River Delta, and remembers seeing her often on her route. During World War II she served as a U.S. Navy ferry, then was brought to the Mississippi River system in 1947 by Tom Greene, the owner of a steamboat line and son of one of the few women steamboat captains, Mary Greene.*

Smoked Trout and Potato Patties
with Horseradish Sauce

⚓

Smoked fish, especially trout and whitefish, are beloved by upriver cooks. Potato pancakes are standards in every Scandinavian cuisine, so it is only natural that smoked fish and potato pancakes have become united, as in these delicious patties. This is Sunday cooking, as welcome as a brunch dish as it is a supper main course.

Makes 8 patties

HORSERADISH SAUCE
¾ cup sour cream
2 scallions, finely chopped
2 tablespoons bottled
  horseradish
¼ teaspoon freshly ground
  black pepper

**SMOKED TROUT AND
POTATO PATTIES**
5 large baking potatoes
  (about 2 pounds), peeled
  and cut into chunks
8 ounces (approximately
  2 fillets) smoked trout
  fillet, skinned, flaked,
  and checked for bones

¾ cup sour cream
2 scallions, finely chopped
2 tablespoons chopped
  parsley, plus additional
  for garnish
¼ cup milk
1 large egg
1 teaspoon salt
¼ teaspoon freshly ground
  black pepper
2 tablespoons vegetable oil
2 tablespoons unsalted
  butter

1. *Make the Horseradish Sauce.* In a medium bowl, combine the sour cream, scallions, horseradish, and pepper. Stir well, cover with plastic wrap, and refrigerate until ready to serve.

2. *Make the Patties.* In a large saucepan of lightly salted water, boil the potatoes over medium-high heat until tender, about 25 minutes. Drain the potatoes well and return them to the saucepan. Stir the potatoes over medium heat until the excess moisture evaporates, about 1 minute. Transfer the potatoes to a large bowl and mash well, using a potato masher, ricer, or hand-held electric mixer until they are a very fine texture.

3. While the potatoes are still warm, beat in the trout, sour cream, scallions, parsley, milk, egg, salt, and pepper. Using about ½ cup of the mixture for each, form patties about 4 inches wide.

4. In a very large skillet or griddle, heat the oil and butter over medium heat. Add the patties and cook, turning them once, until well browned, about 8 to 10 minutes. Transfer them to paper towels to drain briefly. Sprinkle the patties with the parsley and serve immediately with a dollop of the horseradish sauce.

Over 60 percent of the world's supply of horseradish is grown in southern Illinois, across the Mississippi from St. Louis.

Fish Fillets with Bayou Shrimp Stuffing

⚓

Red snapper, once the king of the Mexican Gulf, has been overfished to near extinction, which is why it's so expensive when you do manage to find it at the fish market. Perch is a fine substitute, but be warned that there are some dishonest fishmongers who will charge red snapper prices for the common perch. No matter what fish you use, this spicy shellfish stuffing makes it extra-special.

Makes 4 servings

Nonstick vegetable cooking spray
3 tablespoons unsalted butter, divided
1 medium onion, finely chopped
1 medium celery rib, finely chopped
1 small green bell pepper, seeded and finely chopped
2 scallions, finely chopped
1 garlic clove, minced
2 tablespoons chopped fresh parsley

2 teaspoons Bayou Seasoning (page 46)
1 teaspoon Worcestershire sauce
½ teaspoon salt, divided
8 ounces medium shrimp, peeled, deveined, and cut into ½-inch pieces
1 cup fresh bread crumbs
8 perch fillets (about 1 pound total)
¼ teaspoon freshly ground black pepper
Lemon wedges, for garnish

1. Preheat the oven to 400°F. Lightly spray a 13 × 9-inch baking dish with nonstick cooking spray. In a large skillet, heat 2 tablespoons of the butter over medium heat. Add the onion, celery, green bell pepper, scallion, and garlic. Cook, covered, stirring occasionally, until the vegetables are softened, about 6 minutes. Remove from the heat and stir in the parsley, Bayou Seasoning, Worcestershire sauce, and ¼ teaspoon salt. Stir in the shrimp and bread crumbs.

2. Place 4 of the fillets, skin side down, in the baking dish. Mound one fourth of the filling over each fillet (don't worry that the stuffing doesn't neatly cover the fillets), then cover with the remaining fillets, skin side up. Dot them with the remaining 1 tablespoon butter, then sprinkle with the remaining ¼ teaspoon salt and the pepper.

3. Bake until the fish is just opaque when flaked with a fork, 15 to 20 minutes. Using a spatula, transfer the stuffed fillets to dinner plates and serve immediately with lemon wedges.

Lagniappe: Red snapper fillets are bigger. If you can get them, buy 4 fillets, cut them in half crosswise, and sandwich the stuffing between the two pieces.

Jambalaya Pasta

⚓

Jambalaya, perhaps the most famous of all Creole recipes, is a shellfish-and-pork-studded tomato sauce cooked with rice. There are differing explanations of jambalaya's unique name—for one, that it is related to jamón (Spanish for "ham"), and another, that it is based on a directive made to a Creole cook to mix something up (as in "Jean, balayez!"). Recently, many Louisiana cooks have been mixing up their jambalaya with pasta rather than rice, and the results are excellent. The Creole tomato sauce that forms the backbone of the dish is extremely versatile and used in many classic recipes. Freeze leftover sauce in 1- or 2-cup containers so you'll always have some on hand.

Makes about 7 cups sauce; 4 to 6 servings

CREOLE TOMATO SAUCE
1 tablespoon olive oil
1 large onion, finely chopped
1 medium green bell pepper, seeded and finely chopped
2 celery ribs with leaves, finely chopped
4 scallions, finely chopped
2 garlic cloves, minced
1 28-ounce can crushed tomatoes
1 28-ounce can whole tomatoes in juice, undrained
2 tablespoons chopped fresh parsley
1 tablespoon dried thyme
1 tablespoon dried basil
1 tablespoon dried oregano
1/8 teaspoon ground red pepper
Nonstick vegetable spray
8 ounces Canadian bacon or smoked ham, cut into 1/2-inch pieces
1 pound medium shrimp, peeled and deveined
1 pound dried fettuccine

1. *Make the Sauce.* In a large saucepan, heat the oil over medium heat. Add the onion, bell pepper, and celery. Cover and cook, stirring often, until the vegetables are softened, about 10 minutes. Add the scallions and garlic and cook 1 minute.

2. Stir in the crushed tomatoes, whole tomatoes with their juice, parsley, thyme, basil, oregano, and red pepper. Bring to a simmer over medium-high heat, stirring to break up the whole tomatoes with a spoon. Reduce the heat to low and simmer until thickened and reduced to about 7 cups sauce, about 1 hour. Reserve 4 cups of the sauce, saving the remainder for another use. (The sauce can be prepared up to 3 days ahead, cooled, covered, and refrigerated, or frozen for up to 2 months.)

3. In a large skillet sprayed with nonstick vegetable spray, cook the Canadian bacon over medium heat until lightly browned, about 4 minutes. Add the 4 cups of sauce and bring to a simmer. Add the shrimp and cook until just firm, about 3 minutes. Keep the sauce warm over very low heat.

4. Meanwhile, in a large pot of lightly salted boiling water, cook the pasta until just tender, about 9 minutes. Drain well and return to the empty pot. Pour the sauce over the pasta and mix well. Transfer to a warmed serving bowl and serve immediately.

> **T**omatoes were not eaten in America until well after the
> Revolutionary War, as they were considered poisonous. Italian
> immigrants brought tomatoes to the state of Mississippi,
> where they are now an important crop.

It took a fairly large crew to run a riverboat, and with the time the men spent living aboard the

boat, the cook was without question one of the more important—and popular—members of the staff. Luxury, comfort, and good food attracted a good many businessmen, as did the chance for shore excursions.

Cincinnati Chili Pasta Bake

⚓

Chili is normally considered a Texas dish, but in Cincinnati an ingenious Greek cook seasoned it well with his country's traditional spices of cinnamon, cumin, and allspice and mixed it with pasta to create Cincinnati chili. Now there are scores of chili parlors in the Queen City. I have turned this Ohio favorite into an oven-baked casserole to be served with a crisp green salad topped with crumbled feta cheese and a hot loaf of crusty bread.

Makes 6 to 8 servings

Nonstick vegetable cooking spray
1 pound ground round
2 medium onions, chopped
1 medium celery rib, cut into 1/4-inch pieces
2 garlic cloves, minced
1 tablespoon chili powder
1 teaspoon salt
1/2 teaspoon ground cinnamon
1/2 teaspoon ground cumin
1/2 teaspoon dried basil
1/2 teaspoon dried oregano
1/4 teaspoon ground allspice
1/4 teaspoon freshly ground black pepper

1 28-ounce can peeled tomatoes in purée
1 8-ounce can tomato sauce
1/2 cup beef stock, preferably homemade, or canned beef broth
1 tablespoon red wine vinegar
1 pound tubular pasta, such as penne
1 16-ounce can dark red kidney beans
2 cups (8 ounces) shredded sharp Cheddar cheese
1 cup fresh bread crumbs
1 tablespoon unsalted butter, cut into small pieces

1. Preheat the oven to 350°F. Lightly spray the inside of a 15 × 10-inch baking dish with the nonstick spray.

2. In a large Dutch oven, over medium-high heat, cook the ground beef, onion, celery, and garlic, stirring often to break up the lumps of meat, until the meat loses its pink color, about 5 minutes. Add the chili powder, salt, cinnamon, cumin, basil, oregano, allspice, and pepper. Cook, stirring, for 1 minute.

3. Add the tomatoes with the purée, tomato sauce, beef stock, and vinegar; stir and break up the tomatoes with a large spoon. Bring to a boil, reduce the heat to low, and simmer until thickened, about 1 hour.

4. Meanwhile, in a large saucepan of salted boiling water, cook the pasta until barely tender, about 8 minutes. Drain well and transfer to a large bowl.

5. Add the sauce, kidney beans, and cheese and toss. Pour into the prepared dish, top with the bread crumbs and dot with bits of butter.

6. Bake until the casserole is bubbling and lightly browned on top, about 30 minutes. Serve immediately.

America's first wine industry was in Ohio, supported by the skills of German wine makers who settled there.

Churchill Downs Burgoo

⚓

The origin of the word *burgoo*, an unusual name for a stew, has been attributed to mispronunciations of the words *bulgur*, *barbecue*, and *bird stew*, as well as *ragout*. In any case, most Kentucky cooks agree that burgoo is their state dish. Usually cooked outside for hours and hours in gargantuan quantities, burgoo is dished up to thousands during Derby festivities as well as served at tailgate parties before autumnal football games. If the cooks have game (squirrel, rabbit, and venison being the most popular), it will certainly end up in the pot. Here is my refined, gameless rendition, which must be started a day ahead to allow the married flavors to equal those that are simmered *in plein air* for six or seven hours. Characteristically, my burgoo feeds a crowd (ten, perhaps the perfect number for a Kentucky Derby television party), but not the ten thousand or so eaters that the "Burgoo King," James Looney, used to cook for at the turn of the century. Louisvillians serve it with corn bread, but I like it spooned over mashed potatoes, such as Garlic-Mashed Taters and Swedes (page 110).

Makes 10 servings

2 tablespoons vegetable oil, plus more as needed

2 pounds bone-in beef shank

2 pounds lamb stew meat (neck or shoulder), cut into 1-inch cubes

1 3½-pound chicken, rinsed and patted dry

2 large onions, chopped

3 large carrots, cut into ½-inch-thick rounds

3 medium celery ribs, cut into ½-inch-thick slices

1 large green bell pepper, seeded and cut into 1-inch pieces

3 garlic cloves, minced

1 28-ounce can tomatoes in thick purée

1 quart water

1¾ cups chicken stock, preferably homemade, or low-sodium canned chicken broth

1¾ cups beef stock, preferably homemade, or canned beef broth

3 tablespoons cider vinegar

2 teaspoons dried thyme

2 teaspoons salt

1 teaspoon freshly ground black pepper

½ **teaspoon crushed red pepper flakes or more to taste**

2 cups fresh or defrosted frozen corn kernels

2 cups fresh or defrosted frozen lima beans

2 cups fresh okra, cut into ¼-inch slices

8 tablespoons (1 stick) unsalted butter, softened

½ **cup all-purpose flour**

1 cup chopped fresh parsley

1. In a very large oval casserole or soup pot, heat the oil over medium-high heat. In batches without crowding, brown the beef and lamb, turning occasionally and adding more oil if necessary, until well browned, about 8 minutes per batch. Transfer the browned meat to a plate.

2. Cut the uncooked chicken into 10 pieces: 2 wings, 2 thighs, 2 drumsticks, and 2 breasts which are cut in half crosswise. In batches without crowding, add the chicken to the casserole and cook, turning occasionally, until browned, about 6 minutes. Transfer the chicken to the plate with the beef and lamb.

3. Add the onion, carrot, celery, green bell pepper, and garlic to the fat remaining in the casserole. Cover and cook, stirring occasionally, until softened, about 10 minutes. Return all the meat to the casserole and add the tomatoes, water, chicken and beef stocks, and vinegar. Bring to a simmer, breaking up the tomatoes in the casserole with the side of a spoon and skimming off any foam that rises to the surface. Add the thyme, salt, black pepper, and red pepper.

4. Reduce the heat to low and simmer, covered, until the chicken shows no sign of pink when pierced to the bone, about 45 minutes. Remove the chicken pieces and set aside to cool, then wrap them with plastic wrap and refrigerate until ready to serve the burgoo. Continue to cook the burgoo until the remaining meat is almost tender, about 1 hour to 1 hour and 15 minutes. Add the corn, lima beans, and okra and continue to cook until the meat is completely tender, about 15 minutes. Remove from the heat and allow to cool to room temperature. Cover and refrigerate overnight until ready to serve.

continued

5. The next day, lift off and discard the hardened fat on the surface of the burgoo. Return the chicken to the casserole. Bring the burgoo to a simmer over medium heat, stirring occasionally, about 15 minutes.

6. In a medium bowl, mash the softened butter and flour together with a rubber spatula until a smooth paste is formed. Gradually whisk about 2 cups of the warmed broth from the burgoo into this paste. Gradually stir the mixture back into the burgoo and continue to simmer until the sauce is thickened, about 10 minutes. Stir in the parsley and serve immediately.

This is a recipe from a fund-raiser cookbook, Cruisin' Cuisine *by the American Sternwheel Association, Inc., for Joshua's Foggy Night Chicken. "On foggy night, tie boat up as near voice of farmer's dog as possible. Feed farmer's dog. Acquire 1 farmer's chicken. Return to galley. (Note: On return to galley, acquire 1 dozen farmer's corn if available.) Clean and cut up chicken. Dust chicken in flour. Heat fat in skillet. Fry chicken. Place chicken, 2 cans each cream of celery and cream of mushroom soup and 1½ cans of water in a large pot. Cook over low heat until soup thickens. Serve 6 until fog lifts. Note: If in fog farmer's dog cannot be located, storebought chicken and corn can be substituted for farmer's chicken and corn." (Recipe contributed by Nelson Jones.)*

Braised Short Ribs
with Beer Gravy

⚓

Here's a German-inspired dish that the cooks of St. Louis, Cincinnati, and Pittsburgh might whip up when the breezes off the river turn wintry cold. The gravy is thickened by puréeing the cooked vegetables with the braising juices, so be sure to serve separately prepared vegetables alongside and mashed potatoes or noodles.

Makes 4 to 6 servings

⅓ cup all-purpose flour
1 teaspoon salt
½ teaspoon sweet
   Hungarian paprika
¼ teaspoon freshly ground
   black pepper
8 meaty beef short ribs
   (about 4½ pounds total)
3 tablespoons vegetable
   oil, divided
1 large onion, chopped
2 medium carrots, cut into
   ½-inch-thick rounds

1 medium celery rib with
   leaves, cut into ¼-inch-
   thick slices
2 garlic cloves, minced
1 cup dark beer
½ cup beef broth,
   preferably homemade, or
   canned
1 teaspoon dried thyme
1 bay leaf
Bottled horseradish

1. Preheat the oven to 325°F. Mix the flour, salt, paprika, and pepper on a plate. Roll the short ribs in the mixture and pat well to adhere. Reserve the remaining flour mixture.

2. In a large flameproof Dutch oven, heat 2 tablespoons of the oil over medium-high heat. In batches to avoid crowding, add the short ribs, fat side down. Cook, turning occasionally, until browned on all sides, about 8 minutes. Transfer the short ribs to a plate and set aside. Discard the fat and wipe out the Dutch oven with paper towels.

3. Return the Dutch oven to the stove and heat the remaining 1 tablespoon oil over medium heat. Add the onion, carrot, and celery. Cover and cook, stirring occasionally, until the onion is golden brown, about 8 minutes. Add the garlic and cook for 1 minute. Stir in the beer, beef broth, thyme, and bay leaf; bring to a simmer.

4. Return the short ribs to the Dutch oven. Cover and bake, occasionally turning them, until very tender, 2 to 2½ hours. Transfer the short ribs to a serving platter and cover with foil to keep warm.

5. Skim off and discard the fat from the surface of the cooking liquid, and discard the bay leaf. Transfer the contents of the Dutch oven to a blender, add 2 tablespoons of the reserved flour mixture, and purée. Return the purée to the Dutch oven and bring to a simmer over medium heat. Cook, stirring often, until thickened, about 3 minutes. Season to taste with salt and pepper. Pour into a warm sauceboat and serve the sauce with short ribs, accompanied by horseradish.

Lagniappe: If you wish, substitute additional beef broth for the dark beer.

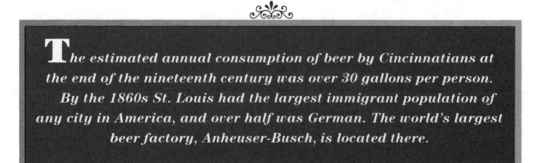

The estimated annual consumption of beer by Cincinnatians at the end of the nineteenth century was over 30 gallons per person. By the 1860s St. Louis had the largest immigrant population of any city in America, and over half was German. The world's largest beer factory, Anheuser-Busch, is located there.

Tugs, *like the J.B. O'Brien, were usually used for pushing huge rafts of timber and coal. But when the ferryboats were out of service they were called upon to transport passengers out to meet passing riverboats. In the dining room of luxury steamboats, formality was the rule. The entire staff took considerable pride in the carefully chosen table settings, sumptuous food, and gracious service.*

Dilled Meatballs with Mushroom Gravy

⚓

Yes, these are "Swedish" meatballs, but a far cry from the canned cream of mushroom soup variety. I put "Swedish" in quotes, for these bite-sized morsels are enjoyed throughout Scandinavia, especially in Finland. American-Scandinavian cooks in the north river regions hotly debate the origin of these, and to call them Swedish in front of a Finnish cook is to invite a pretty violent argument. Set aside the politics, and make these for an informal, hearty family meal.

Makes 4 to 6 servings

1 tablespoon unsalted butter
½ pound fresh mushrooms, sliced
¾ teaspoon salt
½ cup fresh bread crumbs
½ cup heavy cream
1 large egg, beaten
¼ cup minced onion
2 tablespoons chopped fresh dill or 2 teaspoons dried dill
¼ teaspoon ground allspice
¼ teaspoon grated nutmeg

¼ teaspoon freshly ground black pepper
½ pound ground beef
¼ pound ground pork
¼ pound ground veal
1 tablespoon vegetable oil
2 tablespoons all-purpose flour
¾ cup beef broth, preferably homemade, or canned
¾ cup water
Hot cooked egg noodles or rice

1. In a large skillet, melt the butter over medium heat. Add the mushrooms and ¼ teaspoon of the salt. Cook, stirring often, until the mushrooms have given off their liquid and have browned lightly, about 6 minutes. Transfer the mushrooms to a plate and set aside.

2. In a medium bowl, combine the bread crumbs, ¼ cup of the heavy cream, the egg, onion, 1 tablespoon of the dill, the remaining ½ teaspoon salt, allspice, nutmeg, and ⅛ teaspoon of the pepper. Stir with a fork until well mixed. Add the ground meats and mix until well blended. Using about 1 tablespoon of the mixture for each, form meatballs and place them on a waxed paper–lined baking sheet. Refrigerate for 30 minutes.

3. In a large skillet, heat the oil over medium-high heat. Add the meatballs and cook, turning them occasionally, until browned all over, about 8 minutes. Sprinkle the flour over the meatballs and gently turn them until the flour is absorbed. Add the beef broth and water to the pan. Bring to a simmer, scraping up the browned bits from the bottom of the pan with a wooden spoon. Reduce the heat to low, cover, and simmer 5 minutes.

4. Gently stir in the mushrooms, the remaining ¼ cup cream, 1 tablespoon dill, and ⅛ teaspoon pepper. Cook until just heated through, about 2 minutes. Serve over egg noodles or rice.

Lagniappe: Refrigerating the meatballs helps them hold their shape during browning.

Just how long is the Mississippi? The U.S. Army Corps of Engineers measures 2,344 miles long from its source in Lake Itasca, Minnesota, to the Gulf of Mexico. Including the Missouri River (which some consider to be part of the Mississippi), the river is 3,740 miles long, making it the third longest river in the world after the Nile and the Amazon.

Swedish Cup of Coffee
Leg of Lamb

⚓

This Scandinavian specialty may sound like an odd combination, but I assure you that the results are delicious. The sauce is quite rich, with only a spoonful per serving. I always serve this with Jannson's Temptation (page 112) and Green Beans Smothered with Ham and Mushrooms (page 108).

Makes 6 servings

1 4½-pound leg of lamb, preferably butt end, trimmed of excess fat

1 garlic clove, cut into thin slivers

½ teaspoon salt

¼ teaspoon freshly ground black pepper

1 medium onion, sliced

1 medium carrot, cut into ½-inch-thick rounds

1½ cups hot, brewed strong coffee

½ cup half-and-half

1 tablespoon sugar

3 tablespoons unsalted butter

3 tablespoons all-purpose flour

1. Preheat the oven to 450°F. Using the tip of a small sharp knife, cut small slits in the lamb and insert the garlic slivers. Rub the lamb with the salt and pepper and place it on a rack in a flameproof roasting pan.

2. Roast the lamb for 10 minutes. Add the onion and carrot slices to the roasting pan. In a small bowl, stir together the hot coffee, half-and-half, and sugar and pour into the pan. Continue roasting, basting often, allowing 12 minutes per pound (about 50 minutes for a 4½-pound roast), until a meat thermometer inserted into the thickest part of the lamb reads 130°F (medium-rare). Transfer the roast to a serving platter and set aside for 10 minutes before carving.

3. Strain the cooking liquid into a glass bowl and skim off the fat that rises to the surface. Place the roasting pan over two burners. Add the butter and melt over medium-low heat. Whisk in the flour and cook, whisking constantly, for 1 minute. Whisk in the skimmed cooking liquid and cook until thickened, about 3 minutes. Pour the sauce into a warmed sauceboat. Carve the lamb and serve with the sauce alongside.

Smoked Pork Shoulder
with Mustard Sauce

⚓

Smoked pork products are popular the entire length of the river, and perhaps most sought after where the German influence is strongest. Smoked pork shoulder has a taste similar to that of ham, but its modest size makes it attractive to smaller families. A brief water blanching followed by cooking in apple juice tames any excessive saltiness, and renders a broth than can easily be transformed into a luscious mustard sauce.

Makes 4 to 6 servings

1 3-pound smoked pork
   shoulder
1 medium onion, chopped
1 medium carrot, cut into
   ½-inch pieces
1 tablespoon unsalted
   butter
1 cup apple juice
1 cup chicken stock,
   preferably homemade, or
   low-sodium canned
   chicken broth

MUSTARD SAUCE
3 tablespoons unsalted
   butter
3 tablespoons all-purpose
   flour
1½ cups reserved cooking
   liquid
3 tablespoons spicy brown
   German-style mustard

1. Place the pork shoulder in a (preferably oval) casserole just large enough to hold it. Add enough cold water to cover and slowly bring to a simmer over medium-low heat. Drain the pork shoulder. Peel off and discard the netting surrounding it and set aside.

2. In the same casserole, cook the onion and carrot in the butter, covered, over medium-low heat until the vegetables are softened, about 5 minutes. Add the apple juice and chicken stock and bring to a simmer. Return the pork shoulder to the casserole, cover, and simmer over low heat until a meat thermometer inserted into the center of the meat reads 160°F, about 1 hour 30 minutes. Transfer the pork shoulder to a serving platter and cover it loosely with foil to keep warm. Strain the juices through a sieve into a glass bowl,

pressing hard on the solids. Discard the solids and let the juices stand for 5 minutes. Skim off and discard any fat that rises to the surface. Measure 1½ cups of the cooking liquid and reserve.

3. *Make the Sauce.* In a medium saucepan, melt the butter over medium-low heat. Whisk in the flour and let bubble without browning, whisking often, for 2 minutes. Whisk in the reserved cooking liquid, bring to a simmer, and cook, skimming off any foam that floats to the surface, until thickened, about 5 minutes. Remove from the heat and stir in the mustard.

4. Slice the pork shoulder crosswise on the diagonal and serve with the warm mustard sauce.

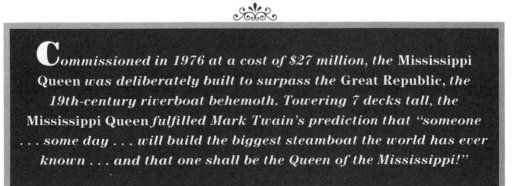

Commissioned in 1976 at a cost of $27 million, the Mississippi Queen was deliberately built to surpass the Great Republic, the 19th-century riverboat behemoth. Towering 7 decks tall, the Mississippi Queen fulfilled Mark Twain's prediction that "someone . . . some day . . . will build the biggest steamboat the world has ever known . . . and that one shall be the Queen of the Mississippi!"

Crescent City Red Beans, Sausage, and Rice

⚓

Practically every restaurant in New Orleans serves red beans and rice on Mondays. Why Monday? In pre–electric appliance days, Monday was laundry day, and this dish could simmer without attention while the cook did the wash. The exact cooking time will vary with the dryness of the beans, so buy yours at a store with a good turnover of its legumes.

Makes 8 servings

1 pound small red chili beans or light kidney beans, rinsed, drained, and picked over
2 tablespoons olive oil
1 pound andouille or kielbasa sausage, cut into ½-inch slices
1 large onion, chopped
1 large celery rib, cut into ½-inch pieces
1 medium green bell pepper, seeded, stemmed, and cut into ½-inch pieces

6 scallions, chopped
2 garlic cloves, minced
3 cups beef broth, preferably homemade, or canned
3 cups water
1 teaspoon dried thyme
½ teaspoon freshly ground black pepper
¼ teaspoon ground hot red (cayenne) pepper
2 bay leaves
½ teaspoon salt
4 cups hot cooked rice

1. In a large soup pot, combine the beans and enough water to cover them by 2 inches. Bring to a boil over high heat and cook for 2 minutes. Remove from the heat, cover, and let stand for 1 hour. Drain well. (The beans can also be soaked overnight in a large bowl with enough cold water to cover by 2 inches, then drained.)

2. In a large soup pot, heat the oil over medium heat. Add the sausage and cook, turning often, until lightly browned, about 5 minutes. With a slotted spoon, transfer the sausage to a plate and set aside.

3. Add the onion, celery, bell pepper, scallion, and garlic to pot. Cover and cook, stirring occasionally, until the vegetables are softened, about 7 minutes. Stir in the beef broth, water, thyme, black and cayenne peppers, and bay leaves. Bring to a boil over high heat.

4. Stir in the drained beans. Reduce the heat to low and simmer, covered, for 30 minutes. Stir in the salt and continue simmering until the beans are just tender, 15 to 30 additional minutes depending on the dryness of the beans. Stir in the sausage and cook for 15 minutes more.

5. Using a potato masher or a large spoon, crush enough of the beans in the pot to thicken the dish to your desired consistency. Serve in bowls, spooned over hot cooked rice.

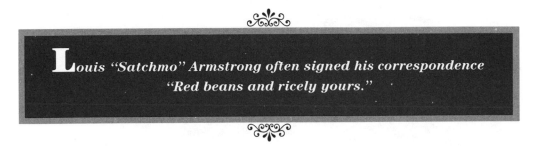

Louis "Satchmo" Armstrong often signed his correspondence "Red beans and ricely yours."

Originally, steamboats had deep hulls, which made them susceptible to snagging onto the tree roots that clogged the rivers. In 1816, Henry Shreve designed the flat-bottomed Washington, which was able to glide

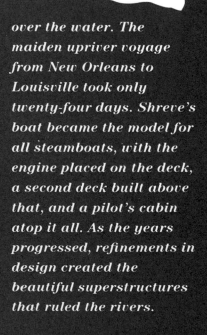

over the water. The maiden upriver voyage from New Orleans to Louisville took only twenty-four days. Shreve's boat became the model for all steamboats, with the engine placed on the deck, a second deck built above that, and a pilot's cabin atop it all. As the years progressed, refinements in design created the beautiful superstructures that ruled the rivers.

Memphis Dry Rub Ribs

⚓

Barbecue, the slow cooking of meats over smoldering hardwood coals, varies from state to state, indeed, from town to town. In Tennessee, however, "real" barbecue is almost always pork, preferably spareribs, smoked over the plentiful hickory wood found throughout the state. Memphis, in particular, has become a mecca for barbecue lovers. This is the best way I know for home cooks to get tender, fall-off-the-bone ribs infused with smoky flavor. With both a spicy dry rub and a slathering of honey-bourbon sauce, these ribs couldn't get more delectable. Don't expect a big hit of bourbon flavor, as the alcohol burns off during the simmering; rather think of it as a stabilizer for the different ingredients, much like alcohol works in extracts and perfumes.

Makes 6 to 8 servings

DRY RUB
¼ cup chili powder
2 tablespoons garlic salt
2 tablespoons onion powder
2 tablespoons paprika, preferably sweet Hungarian
2 tablespoons freshly ground black pepper
2 teaspoons cayenne pepper
6 pounds spareribs

HONEY-BOURBON BBQ SAUCE
4 tablespoons (½ stick) unsalted butter

1 large onion, finely chopped
2 garlic cloves, minced
1 cup catsup
1 cup chili sauce
½ cup honey
½ cup lemon juice
⅓ cup bourbon or apple juice
2 tablespoons prepared brown mustard
2 tablespoons Worcestershire sauce
¼ teaspoon cayenne pepper

2 cups hickory chips

1. *Make the Dry Rub.* In a small bowl, combine all the ingredients. Rub the mixture on both sides of the spareribs. Wrap them tightly in aluminum foil and let them stand at room temperature for 1 hour, or refrigerate them for 4 hours, or up to overnight.

2. *Make the BBQ Sauce.* In a medium heavy-bottomed saucepan, heat the butter over medium heat. Add the onion and garlic and cook, stirring often, until softened, about 5 minutes. Stir in the remaining ingredients. Bring to a simmer, reduce the heat to low, and cook, stirring often to avoid scorching, until thickened, about 1 hour.

3. Soak the hickory chips in cold water to cover for at least 30 minutes. Drain and set aside.

4. Make a hot charcoal fire in a regular grill (using about 35 briquettes) or preheat a gas grill to low. When the coals are covered with white ash, place the wrapped ribs on the grill and cook, turning often, for about 1 hour. Carefully unwrap the ribs and check for tenderness by piercing them with a knife. They should be almost tender. (If not, rewrap and continue cooking.) Set the unwrapped ribs aside, loosely covered. (You may pour off the juices, skim off the fat, and stir them into the BBQ sauce if you want.)

5. Meanwhile, in a hibachi or portable grill, make another charcoal fire (using about 15 briquettes). Add the ash-covered hot coals from this to the larger charcoal grill. (I use pot holders to remove the grill grate and a garden spade to transfer the coals from the smaller grill.) Sprinkle the coals with the hickory chips. (If using a gas grill, wrap the chips in aluminum foil packets, pierce the packets all over with the tip of a knife, and place the packets directly on the heat source or rocks.) Return the ribs to the grill and brush both sides with the BBQ sauce. Cover and cook for 10 minutes until the sauce is glazed but not burned. Turn, slather the ribs with more sauce, and continue cooking for another 10 minutes, until the spareribs are tender. Cut the ribs between the bones and serve immediately.

The first white explorer to see the Mississippi River was the Spaniard Hernando de Soto in 1541, a few miles south of today's Memphis. He was on an expedition from the Florida territory to discover gold and treasure and was hardly aware of the importance of his discovery. He died a few months later, and by the time the survivors of the expedition returned, they had traveled over 350,000 square miles in four years.

Cajun Meat Pies

⚓

In bayou country, meat pies can be found for sale just about anywhere—roadside stands, bakeries, gas stations, even a restaurant or two. Their popularity can be understood at first bite—flaky pastry turnovers with a spicy ground meat filling. They make a hearty lunch and they are great picnic fare too.

Makes 6 pies

FLAKY PASTRY DOUGH
2 cups all-purpose flour
½ teaspoon salt
⅔ cup lard or vegetable shortening, chilled and cut into small pieces
About ½ cup ice water

FILLING
½ pound ground round
1 medium onion, finely chopped
1 celery rib, finely chopped
2 scallions, chopped
1 small green bell pepper, finely chopped

1 garlic clove, minced
1½ tablespoons Bayou Seasoning (page 46)
⅓ cup beef broth
1 tablespoon tomato paste
1 tablespoon Worcestershire sauce
½ teaspoon salt

1 egg beaten with 1 teaspoon milk to make a glaze

1. *Make the Dough.* In a medium bowl, combine the flour and salt. Using a pastry blender or two knives, cut the lard into the flour until the mixture resembles small peas. Tossing the mixture with a fork, gradually sprinkle in the ice water until the dough is moist enough to hold together when pinched between your thumb and forefinger. (You may have to add a little more ice water.) Gather the dough into a thick, flat disk, wrap it in waxed paper, and refrigerate at least 1 hour, or overnight.

2. *Make the Filling.* Preheat the oven to 400°F. In a large skillet, cook the ground round, onion, celery, scallion, bell pepper, and garlic over medium-high heat, stirring often to break up the lumps of meat, until the meat loses its pink color, about 5 minutes. Add the Bayou Seasoning and stir for 30 seconds. Stir in the beef broth, tomato paste, Worcestershire sauce, and salt. Cook, stirring often, until thickened, about 3 minutes. Remove from the heat and cool completely.

3. On a lightly floured surface, roll out the dough to ⅛ inch thick. Using a 6-inch saucer as a guide, cut out 6 circles, gathering up dough scraps and re-rolling as necessary. Place about ⅓ cup cooled filling on the lower half of a dough circle. Brush the edge of the circle with some egg glaze and fold in half to enclose the filling. Press the edges together and seal with the tines of a fork. Pierce the top of the turnover with the fork to allow steam to escape. Place on an ungreased baking sheet. Repeat with the remaining dough and filling.

4. Lightly brush the pies with egg glaze. Bake until golden brown, about 20 minutes. Serve hot, warm, or at room temperature.

A slang term that comes from the riverboat days is riffraff. Early river travelers floated downriver on a raft that was propelled by oars called "rifs." As steamboat voyages became more popular and elegant, only poor folks used the "rif rafts," and eventually they took on the name of their mode of travel.

ROUNDIN' THE BEND:

SALADS AND SIDE DISHES

Muffuletta Salad

⚓

This is certainly one of the tastiest ways to use up day-old bread that I know. And it is truly a memorable sensory experience when you use leftover garlic bread—just be sure your guests are all garlic lovers! To make this heartier (and a bit closer to the New Orleans sandwiches the salad is named after), add 1 cup each of finely chopped salami, mozzarella cheese, and boiled ham.

Makes 8 servings

OLIVE SALAD

- 1 cup pimiento-stuffed green olives, thinly sliced
- 1 cup ripe pitted black olives, thinly sliced
- 2 celery ribs, thinly sliced
- ¼ cup chopped parsley
- ¼ cup red wine vinegar
- 2 garlic cloves, minced
- ¼ teaspoon salt
- ¼ teaspoon crushed hot red pepper flakes
- ¾ cup olive oil, preferably extra-virgin

- ½ loaf day-old French, Italian, or garlic bread, cut into ½-inch pieces (about 4 cups)
- Head of romaine, rinsed, dried, and torn into bite-sized pieces
- Head of red leaf lettuce, rinsed, dried, and torn into bite-sized pieces
- 6 medium plum tomatoes, cut into ½-inch pieces
- 1 Vidalia or white onion, thinly sliced
- 2 Kirby cucumbers, scrubbed and cut into ½-inch pieces

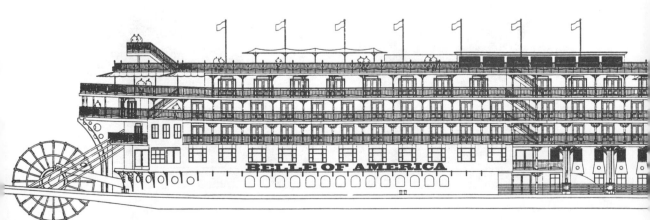

1. *Make the Olive Salad.* In a medium bowl, combine the sliced green and black olives, celery, and parsley. In another bowl, whisk the red wine vinegar, garlic, salt, and red pepper flakes. Gradually whisk in the olive oil. Pour half of the dressing (reserve the remaining dressing) over the olive mixture and mix well. Cover the olive salad and refrigerate for at least 4 hours, preferably overnight. (The olive salad and the dressing can be prepared up to 3 days ahead, covered tightly and refrigerated.)

2. Place the bread in a large salad bowl and add the olive salad. Toss well and let stand for 5 minutes. Add the lettuces, tomato, onion slices, and cucumber. Whisk the remaining dressing, drizzle over the salad, and toss well. Serve immediately.

Lagniappe: An easy way to slice the olives is to use a food processor fitted with the thin slicing blade. With the machine running, drop the olives through the feed tube.

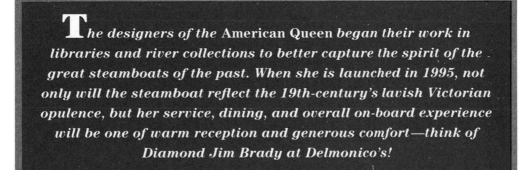

The designers of the American Queen began their work in libraries and river collections to better capture the spirit of the great steamboats of the past. When she is launched in 1995, not only will the steamboat reflect the 19th-century's lavish Victorian opulence, but her service, dining, and overall on-board experience will be one of warm reception and generous comfort—think of Diamond Jim Brady at Delmonico's!

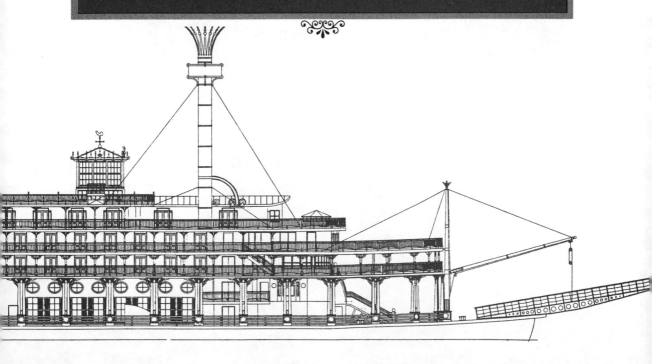

Scarlet Poppy Seed Salad Dressing

⚓

Throughout the Midwest, thick, sweet salad dressings the colors of Day-Glo paints are poured out of bottles over crisp iceberg lettuce. Now I admit that I like this kind of salad occasionally, so I devised this ruby-colored dressing from puréed fresh raspberries. I think you'll find it far superior to the bottled varieties. Serve it over a simple mixture of romaine, tomato wedges, and red onion.

Makes 1¹/₂ cups

¹/₂ **pint fresh raspberries**	**1 teaspoon dry mustard**
³/₄ **cup vegetable oil**	¹/₂ **teaspoon salt**
¹/₄ **cup cider vinegar**	¹/₄ **teaspoon freshly ground**
¹/₄ **cup orange juice**	**black pepper**
1 teaspoon sugar	**2 tablespoons poppy seeds**

1. In a food processor fitted with a metal blade or a blender, purée the raspberries and strain through a fine sieve to remove the seeds. Return the purée to the food processor and add the oil, vinegar, orange juice, sugar, mustard, salt, and pepper. Blend until smooth and thickened, about 30 seconds. Add the poppy seeds and pulse briefly. Serve as a salad dressing. (The dressing can be prepared up to 3 days ahead, covered tightly and refrigerated. Shake well before serving.)

The term mark twain *refers to a river depth of twelve feet, the clearance needed for a steamboat's draft. Samuel Clemens was a riverboat pilot and took his pen name from this.*

The Hill Potato and Artichoke Salad

⚓

St. Louis' Italian community is centered on the Hill, a barely elevated area in the center of the city. This sensational chunky potato salad is made the Italian way with marinated artichoke hearts. The denizens of the Hill would flavor the salad with basil, but simply use whatever *fresh* herbs you have handy.

Makes 8 to 12 servings

3 tablespoons white wine
 vinegar
2 garlic cloves, crushed
½ teaspoon salt
¼ teaspoon freshly ground
 black pepper
⅔ cup olive oil
2 10-ounce packages
 defrosted frozen
 artichoke hearts

3 pounds small new
 potatoes, scrubbed
½ cup sour cream or plain
 low-fat yogurt
½ cup mayonnaise
4 scallions, finely chopped
½ cup chopped fresh basil,
 tarragon, dill, or parsley

1. In a medium bowl, whisk together the vinegar, garlic, ¼ teaspoon salt, and ⅛ teaspoon pepper. Gradually whisk in the oil. Add the artichoke hearts and toss well. Cover and refrigerate, stirring occasionally, for at least 4 hours, or overnight.

2. In a large pot of lightly salted boiling water, cook the potatoes over high heat until tender, about 20 minutes. Drain them well and rinse under cold water until cool enough to handle. Peel the potatoes, if desired, and slice them thickly into a large bowl.

3. In a medium bowl, fold together the sour cream, mayonnaise, scallions, and basil. Pour over the potatoes. Add the artichoke hearts with their marinade, the remaining ¼ teaspoon salt and ⅛ teaspoon pepper; toss well. Cover with plastic wrap and chill for at least 2 hours.

4. When ready to serve, reseason with additional salt and pepper to taste. Serve the salad chilled.

Apple Orchard Coleslaw

⚓

Upper-river cooks have an abundance of apples, which sustained many a pioneer family in many ways—sliced and fried, strung up and left out to dry in the sun, eaten fresh in hand, turned into applesauce, grated and baked into a cake, squeezed into cider, and fermented into applejack. Here, shredded fresh apples and apple butter add a sweet-tangy note to a creamy slaw.

Makes 8 servings

2/3 cup sour cream

1/3 cup mayonnaise

1/3 cup unsweetened apple butter

2 tablespoons cider vinegar

1 teaspoon caraway seeds, crushed (optional)

1 teaspoon salt

1/4 teaspoon freshly ground black pepper

5 cups (about 1 1/4 pounds) shredded green cabbage

2 medium tart apples, such as Granny Smith, peeled, cored, and shredded

3 medium carrots, shredded

2 scallions, finely chopped

1. In a large bowl, stir the sour cream, mayonnaise, apple butter, vinegar, caraway seeds, salt, and pepper until smooth. Add the cabbage, apples, carrots, and scallions and toss well. Cover and refrigerate for at least 1 hour before serving.

Lagniappe: If you wish, use nonfat sour cream and reduced-fat mayonnaise to make a low-fat variation of this popular picnic standard.

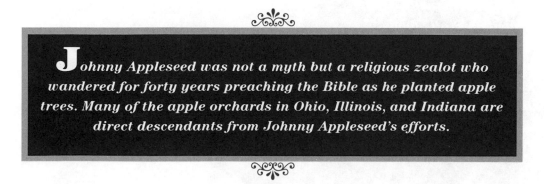

*J*ohnny Appleseed was not a myth but a religious zealot who wandered for forty years preaching the Bible as he planted apple trees. Many of the apple orchards in Ohio, Illinois, and Indiana are direct descendants from Johnny Appleseed's efforts.

The landing of a
riverboat caused quite a
stir in small towns along
the river. Some boats
brought cotton, coal, and
other necessities, while
others dealt in luxury
items such as exotic foods,
fashionable clothes, and
fine furnishings. But
perhaps most important,
steamboats, especially the
luxury boats, brought an
influx of people and new
ideas.

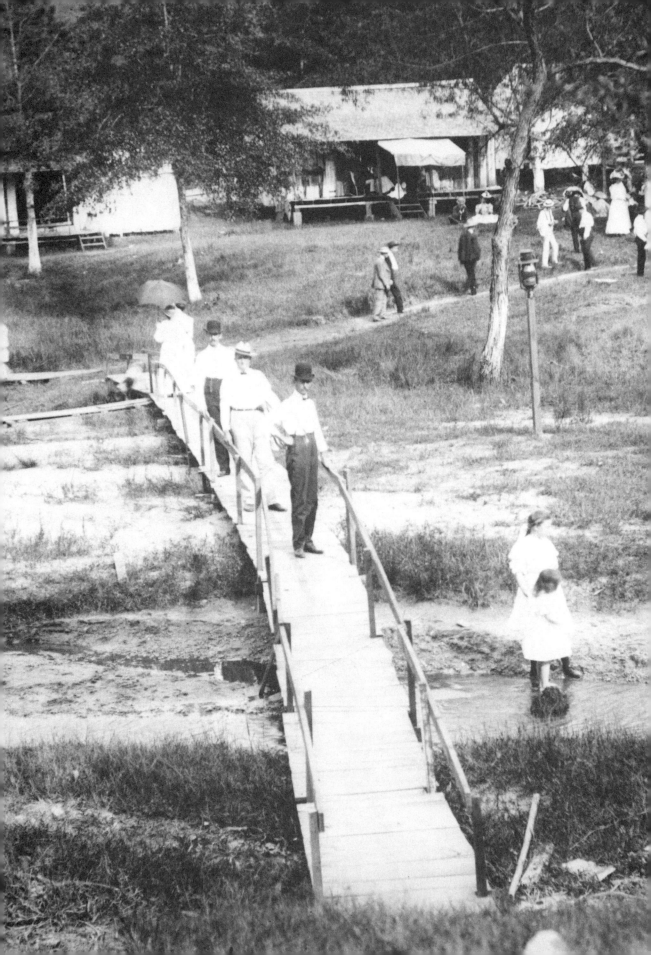

Macaroni and Blue Cheese Salad

⚓

In the town of Nauvoo, Illinois, tangy blue-veined cheese is aged in limestone caves which overlook the Mississippi River. While it is a world-class cheese, southwestern Illinois cooks take it for granted and use it in simple recipes like this—the kind of macaroni (not "pasta") salad that you might find at a Nauvoo church picnic or little league fund-raiser.

Makes 6 to 8 servings

8 ounces dried macaroni, such as elbow or ditali

2 celery ribs, chopped into ¼-inch pieces

3 scallions, chopped

2 tablespoons vinegar, preferably white wine vinegar

4 ounces blue cheese, crumbled

¾ cup mayonnaise

6 tablespoons heavy cream, plus more as needed

¼ teaspoon freshly ground black pepper

Salt to taste

¼ cup chopped parsley

1. In a large pot of lightly salted boiling water, cook the macaroni until just tender, about 8 minutes. Drain, rinse under cold water, and drain well. Transfer to a medium bowl and add the celery and scallions. Sprinkle with the vinegar and toss well.

2. In a small bowl, combine the blue cheese, mayonnaise, heavy cream, and pepper. Pour over the macaroni and toss well. Cover and refrigerate for at least 2 hours, or overnight.

3. When ready to serve, stir in additional heavy cream if the salad dressing seems too thick. Season lightly with salt and additional pepper to taste. Sprinkle with parsley and serve chilled.

Lagniappe: Nauvoo Blue Cheese is available by mail order from Nauvoo Mill and Bakery, Route 1, P.O. Box 24, Nauvoo, IL 62354 (217-453-6734). No shipments are made between April and October due to warm weather.

Hoppin' John Salad

⚓

Hoppin' John, probably named for its originator, a cook with a limp, is a hot black-eyed peas and rice dish.

Makes 8 servings

1 pound black-eyed peas
2 teaspoons salt, divided
1 cup long-grain white rice
8 ounces ham, cut into
   ½-inch cubes
1 sweet red bell pepper,
   seeded, stemmed, and cut
   into ¼-inch pieces
4 scallions, chopped

¼ cup chopped fresh
   parsley
¼ cup red wine vinegar
1 garlic clove, minced
1 teaspoon sugar
½ teaspoon crushed hot
   red pepper flakes
¾ cup olive oil

1. In a large pot of boiling water, cook the peas over medium heat for 15 minutes. Add 1 teaspoon of salt and continue cooking until the peas are just tender, about 20 minutes. Drain, rinse under cold water, and drain again. Transfer the peas to a large bowl.

2. In a large saucepan of lightly salted boiling water, cook the rice over medium heat until just tender, 15 to 20 minutes. Drain, rinse with cold water, and drain again. Add the rice, ham, red bell pepper, scallions, and parsley to the peas and toss gently.

3. In a small bowl, whisk the vinegar, garlic, sugar, the remaining 1 teaspoon salt, and crushed pepper. Gradually whisk in the oil.

4. Pour half the dressing over the peas and rice and toss to mix. Cover and refrigerate the salad and remaining dressing for 2 hours, or overnight. Just before serving, add remaining dressing and mix well.

Lagniappe: Substitute 3 16-ounce cans of drained black-eyed peas.

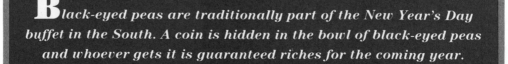

Black-eyed peas are traditionally part of the New Year's Day buffet in the South. A coin is hidden in the bowl of black-eyed peas and whoever gets it is guaranteed riches for the coming year.

Wild Rice and Dried Cherries Salad

⚓

The exact cooking time of wild rice, as for beans, is hard to estimate—it depends on the dryness of the kernels—so check often to be sure it is cooked to your desired doneness. Some like their wild rice slightly resilient, others when it is "puffed" and quite tender. Celery adds crunch and dried cherries contribute tang to this elegant salad.

Makes 6 to 8 servings

1½ cups (9 ounces) wild rice, well rinsed and drained
2 celery ribs, thinly sliced
4 scallions, finely chopped
¼ cup (about 3 ounces) pitted dried cherries

¼ cup cider vinegar
½ teaspoon salt
¼ teaspoon freshly ground black pepper
¾ cup vegetable oil

1. In a large saucepan of lightly salted boiling water, stir in the rice. Cook, uncovered, until the rice is very tender, adding more boiling water if necessary to keep the rice covered, about 1 hour to 1 hour 15 minutes. Drain well, rinse with cold water, and drain again. Transfer the rice to a large bowl, add the celery, scallions, and dried cherries and toss.

2. In a small bowl, whisk the vinegar, salt, and pepper. Gradually whisk in the oil until thickened. Pour half the dressing over the rice and toss well. Cover the bowl with plastic wrap and refrigerate 2 hours, or overnight. Just before serving, add the remaining dressing and toss again. Serve chilled or at room temperature.

Lagniappe: Dried cherries are available by mail order from American Spoon Foods, Inc., P.O. Box 566, Petoskey, MI 49770–0566 (1-800-222-5886) and Williams-Sonoma, P.O. Box 7456, San Francisco, CA 94120-7456 (1-800-541-2233). You can substitute dried cranberries, blueberries, chopped apricots, or golden raisins.

A Mess of Greens

⚓

Boiled greens are only as good as their "pot likker," the cooking liquid in which they are simmered to melting tenderness. Therefore, my pot likker is fortified with bacon, meat stock, celery, carrots, and garlic. These ingredients create a broth that is delicious enough on its own to be used as a dunk for corn bread slices or to sip as a nutritious pick-me-up.

Makes 4 to 6 servings

4 pounds greens, such as turnip, dandelion, kale, or collard, in any combination

4 bacon slices (about 2 ounces)

1 medium onion, chopped

1 medium carrot, cut into ¼-inch pieces

1 medium celery rib, cut into ¼-inch pieces

3 garlic cloves, minced

1¾ cups beef stock, preferably homemade, use canned broth

2 tablespoons cider vinegar

½ teaspoon crushed red pepper flakes

Salt to taste

1. In a large sink of lukewarm water, agitate the greens well to loosen any grit. Carefully lift the greens out of the water and transfer them to a large bowl, leaving any grit on the bottom of the sink. Repeat in a sink of fresh water. Discard the thick stems and chop the greens coarsely.

2. In a large Dutch oven over medium-high heat, cook the bacon, turning once, until crisp, about 5 minutes. With a slotted spoon, transfer the bacon to paper towels, leaving the bacon fat in the Dutch oven. Add the onion, carrot, celery, and garlic and cook over medium-low heat, stirring often, until the vegetables are softened, about 6 minutes. Stir in the beef stock, vinegar, and crushed red pepper and bring to a simmer. Add the greens in batches, covering the pan and waiting for each batch to wilt before adding the next batch. Cover and cook, stirring occasionally, until the greens are very tender, about 1 hour 15 minutes. Season with salt to taste.

3. With a slotted spoon, transfer the greens to a warm serving bowl. Crumble the bacon and sprinkle it over the greens.

Toward the turn of the century, it became quite fashionable to have weddings and other parties aboard the J.M. White *and other luxurious steamboats. Built in 1878, the* J.M. White *was considered the most splendid of all the steamboats. Its ornately furnished main cabin, with its Victorian details, certainly rivaled the most opulent hotels of the day. Sadly, the boat burned in 1886, signaling the beginning of the end of luxury steamboating.*

Green Beans Smothered with Ham and Mushrooms

⚓

While I occasionally enjoy bright emerald, crisp green beans, more often I cook them the old-fashioned way: long-simmered to tenderness, sacrificing vibrant color for depth of taste. Wild mushrooms are found throughout the headwaters region, and even though the ones you buy at your local market may be Italian, the spirit will be the same. These beans are infused with the earthy flavor of mushrooms and seasoned with the sweet, meaty taste of ham.

Makes 6 to 8 servings

½ ounce (about ½ cup) dried wild mushrooms, such as porcini
½ cup boiling water
3 ounces (about ½ cup) ham, cut into ¼-inch dice
1 small onion, chopped
1 tablespoon unsalted butter

10 ounces fresh mushrooms, such as cremini or portobello, rinsed and cut into ½-inch pieces
1 pound green beans, trimmed and cut into 1½-inch lengths
½ teaspoon salt
¼ teaspoon freshly ground black pepper

1. Rinse the dried mushrooms under cold water to loosen the grit. Place them in a small bowl and cover with the boiling water. Let stand until softened, 20 to 30 minutes. Lift the mushrooms from the water, rinse again, and chop coarsely. Set the mushrooms aside. Strain the soaking liquid through a paper towel–lined sieve to remove the grit, reserving the liquid.

2. In a large skillet over low heat, heat the butter. Add the ham and onion and cook until the onion is soft, about 5 minutes. Add the fresh mushrooms and continue to cook until they give off their juices and begin to brown, another 5 minutes.

3. Add the green beans, wild mushrooms, reserved soaking liquid, salt, and pepper. Cover and simmer until the beans are tender and have absorbed the juices, about 30 minutes.

Lagniappe: Cremini and portobello mushrooms are cultivated, not wild, mushrooms, although they retain much of the musky flavor of the wild varieties. Regular white button mushrooms may be substituted.

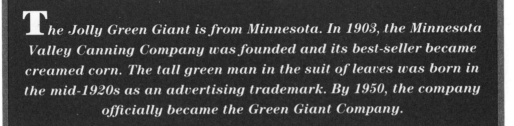

The Jolly Green Giant is from Minnesota. In 1903, the Minnesota Valley Canning Company was founded and its best-seller became creamed corn. The tall green man in the suit of leaves was born in the mid-1920s as an advertising trademark. By 1950, the company officially became the Green Giant Company.

Garlic-Mashed Taters and Swedes

⚓

Root vegetables sustained many settlers during many cold winters. These days, they are popular with city dwellers as well as country folks, who appreciate their earthy flavors. The yellow rutabaga (or Swedish turnip) is as popular in the upper Mississippi region as it is in Scandinavia, where Finnish cooks use it so often one wonders why it isn't called the Finnish turnip. Don't be afraid of the large amount of garlic here; boiling it tames its strength.

Makes 6 to 8 servings

2½ pounds rutabaga, pared and cut into 1-inch cubes

4 medium boiling potatoes (about 2 pounds), peeled and cut into 1-inch cubes

1 garlic head, separated into cloves and peeled

½ cup half-and-half or light cream

3 tablespoons unsalted butter

¼ teaspoon salt

¼ teaspoon freshly ground black pepper

1. In a large pot of lightly salted water, cook the rutabaga, potatoes, and garlic over medium heat until just tender, 20 to 30 minutes. Drain well and return to the pot.

2. Using a hand-held electric mixer or potato masher, mash the vegetables with the half-and-half, butter, salt, and pepper to desired consistency. Transfer to a warm serving dish and serve immediately.

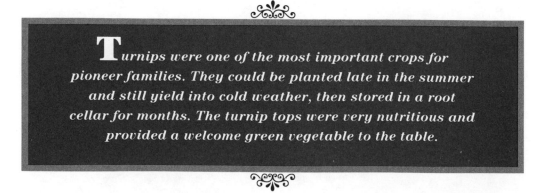

Turnips were one of the most important crops for pioneer families. They could be planted late in the summer and still yield into cold weather, then stored in a root cellar for months. The turnip tops were very nutritious and provided a welcome green vegetable to the table.

Spicy Oven Fries

⚓

All cooks need a simple potato recipe in their repertoire, and this is one of my favorites. It gives the crisp texture of French fries without all the fat and is nicely flavored with a good dash of Bayou Seasoning.

Makes 4 to 6 servings

2 large baking potatoes (about 1 pound 4 ounces), such as Idaho or russet, scrubbed
2 tablespoons canola oil

2 teaspoons Bayou Seasoning (page 46)
¾ teaspoon salt

1. Preheat the oven to 375°F. Using a sharp knife, cut the potatoes into fries, about 5 × ¾ × ½ inch. In a large bowl, toss the potatoes with the oil, Bayou Seasoning, and salt.

2. Spread the potato slices on a shallow baking sheet. Bake, turning them often, until tender and golden brown, 50 to 60 minutes. Serve immediately.

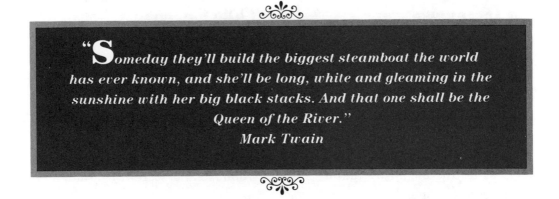

"Someday they'll build the biggest steamboat the world has ever known, and she'll be long, white and gleaming in the sunshine with her big black stacks. And that one shall be the Queen of the River."
Mark Twain

Jannson's Temptation

⚓

Erik Janson was a Swedish religious fanatic who founded an enclave called Bishop's Hill in Illinois in the 1800s. Legend says that although Janson preached against the pleasures of the flesh, this creamy scalloped potato and onion dish was too strong a temptation for even the straightlaced minister. While this story is acceptable, it doesn't explain how the dish traveled back to Scandinavia to become as popular there as mashed potatoes are here, or how the spelling was changed to Jannson. (Another tale credits the invention to a famous opera singer, Adolf Jannson, born Janzon.) Scandinavian-American cooks use Swedish marinated anchovy sprats, which are difficult to find here outside of Swedish-owned delicatessens. I have devised a method to transform supermarket anchovy fillets, and the results are excellent—and *not* just for anchovy lovers.

Makes 6 to 8 servings

4 tablespoons (½ stick) unsalted butter, softened and divided

1 tablespoon cider vinegar

1 tablespoon water

1 teaspoon sugar

1 2-ounce tin anchovy fillets packaged in oil, separated and rinsed

3 small onions, sliced

4 large baking potatoes (about 2 pounds), such as russets, peeled

1 teaspoon salt

¼ teaspoon freshly ground black pepper

2 cups heavy cream, scalded

½ cup fresh bread crumbs

1. Preheat the oven to 350°F. Butter an 11 × 7-inch baking dish with 1 tablespoon of the butter. In a small bowl, whisk together the vinegar, water, and sugar. Add the anchovies and let stand at room temperature for 30 minutes. Drain before using.

2. In a large skillet, heat 2 tablespoons of the remaining butter over medium heat. Add the onion slices and cook, stirring often, until soft but not browned, about 6 minutes.

3. Using a sharp knife or a mandoline slicer, cut the potatoes into 2 × ¼-inch sticks. In the prepared baking dish, layer half of the potatoes, half of the salt and pepper, and all of the onion slices and anchovies. Cover with the rest of the potatoes and salt and pepper. Pour the heavy cream over all, sprinkle with the bread crumbs, and dot with the remaining 1 tablespoon butter.

4. Place the dish on a baking sheet and bake until the bread crumbs are golden brown and the potatoes are tender, about 1 hour. Let stand 5 minutes before serving.

Lagniappe: To julienne the potatoes, use a hand-slicing appliance, such as a mandoline. Mandolines used to be available imported only from France and were very expensive. Most houseware stores now carry inexpensive Swiss-made mandolines that come with a variety of slicing blades.

"**A**nd Thames and all the rivers of the kings
Ran into the Mississippi and were drowned."
Stephen Vincent Benét

Cider-Candied Sweet Potatoes

⚓

Outside of the South, sweet potato dishes are normally reserved for holiday menus. However, on Southern tables they are a year-round staple.

Makes 6 to 8 servings

2 cups fresh-pressed apple
 cider
1½ cups honey
Grated zest of 1 lemon
4 tablespoons lemon juice
3 tablespoons unsalted
 butter

½ teaspoon ground
 cinnamon
½ teaspoon ground
 allspice
¼ teaspoon ground nutmeg
6 medium sweet potatoes
 (Louisiana yams), peeled
 and sliced crosswise into
 ¾-inch rounds

1. In a deep medium saucepan, bring the cider, honey, lemon zest, lemon juice, butter, cinnamon, allspice, and nutmeg to a simmer over medium heat and cook for 10 minutes. Add the sweet potatoes and partially cover. (Add more cider if needed, to barely cover the sweet potatoes.) Simmer over medium-low heat until the sweet potatoes are just tender but not falling apart, about 45 minutes.

2. Using a slotted spoon, carefully transfer the sweet potatoes to a warm serving bowl and cover with foil to keep warm. Increase the heat to high and boil the cider mixture until thickened and evaporated to about 1 cup, 5 to 8 minutes. Pour the hot syrup over the sweet potatoes and serve immediately.

Sweet-and-Sour Spiced Swedish Beans

⚓

These stove-top beans feature a delectable, thick, sweet-and-sour sauce mildly spiced with ginger and cinnamon. As with many upriver Scandinavian dishes, it may seem at its best during cold winter months, but it is equally fitting at a summer picnic table.

Makes 8 to 10 servings

1 pound dried Swedish brown beans or pink kidney beans	**3 tablespoons unsalted butter**
½ cup honey	**2 teaspoons ground ginger**
½ cup packed light brown sugar	**½ teaspoon salt**
⅓ cup cider vinegar	**1 cinnamon stick**

1. In a large pot, combine the beans and enough cold water to cover them by 2 inches. Bring to a boil over high heat and boil for 2 minutes. Remove the pot from the heat, cover, and let stand for 1 hour; drain well. (The beans can also be soaked overnight in a large bowl with enough water to cover by 2 inches, then drained.)

2. Return the beans to the pot and add enough fresh water to cover them by 2 inches. Bring to a boil over high heat, reduce the heat to low, and simmer, partially covered, until the beans are almost tender, about 1 hour. Add boiling water if necessary to keep the beans covered with water during cooking. (The time necessary to cook the beans will vary according to the dryness of the beans.)

3. Stir in the honey, brown sugar, vinegar, butter, ginger, salt, and cinnamon stick. Continue cooking, uncovered, until the beans are completely tender and a thick sauce is formed, about 30 minutes. Add water if necessary during the cooking if the sauce becomes too thick. Or increase the heat to high to thicken the sauce if it seems too thin when the beans are tender. Serve the beans hot.

Lagniappe: Dried Swedish brown beans are available by mail order from Inglebretsen's, 1601 East Lake Street, Minneapolis, MN 55407 (612-729-9331).

Minnesota Wild Rice and Wild Mushrooms

⚓

Celebrating and combining two favorite upriver specialties, wild mushrooms and wild rice, this dish is perfect for very special dinners. I serve it often with game birds, turkey, and roast pork.

Makes 6 to 8 servings

½ ounce (about ½ cup) dried wild mushrooms, such as porcini
1 cup boiling water
2 tablespoons (¼ stick) unsalted butter
1 medium carrot, finely chopped
2 medium celery ribs, finely chopped
¼ cup shallots or scallions, minced
8 ounces fresh mushrooms, such as portobello or cremini

¼ cup chopped parsley
½ teaspoon dried thyme
½ teaspoon salt
¼ teaspoon freshly ground black pepper
1½ cups (9 ounces) wild rice, well rinsed and drained
3½ cups chicken stock, preferably homemade, or canned chicken broth

1. Rinse the dried mushrooms under cold water to loosen the grit. Place them in a small bowl and cover with the boiling water. Let stand until softened, 20 to 30 minutes. Lift the mushrooms from the water, rinse again, and chop coarsely. Set the mushrooms aside. Strain the soaking liquid through a paper towel–lined sieve to remove the grit, reserving the liquid.

2. In a medium saucepan, heat the butter over medium heat. Add the carrot, celery, and shallots, cover, and cook until softened, about 5 minutes. Add the fresh mushrooms, parsley, thyme, salt, and pepper and cook, uncovered, until the mushrooms give off their liquid, it evaporates, and they begin to brown, about 5 minutes.

3. Stir in the wild rice, chicken stock, wild mushrooms, and reserved soaking liquid. Bring to a boil and reduce the heat to medium-low. Cover and cook until the wild rice is tender and the liquid is absorbed, 1 hour to 1 hour 20 minutes. (There may be some unabsorbed liquid. Drain the rice, if desired.) Transfer to a warm serving bowl and serve immediately.

> **T**he tall steam stacks on a stern-wheeler are often too high to go under bridges. Most have a knee joint that allows the stacks to be tilted back.

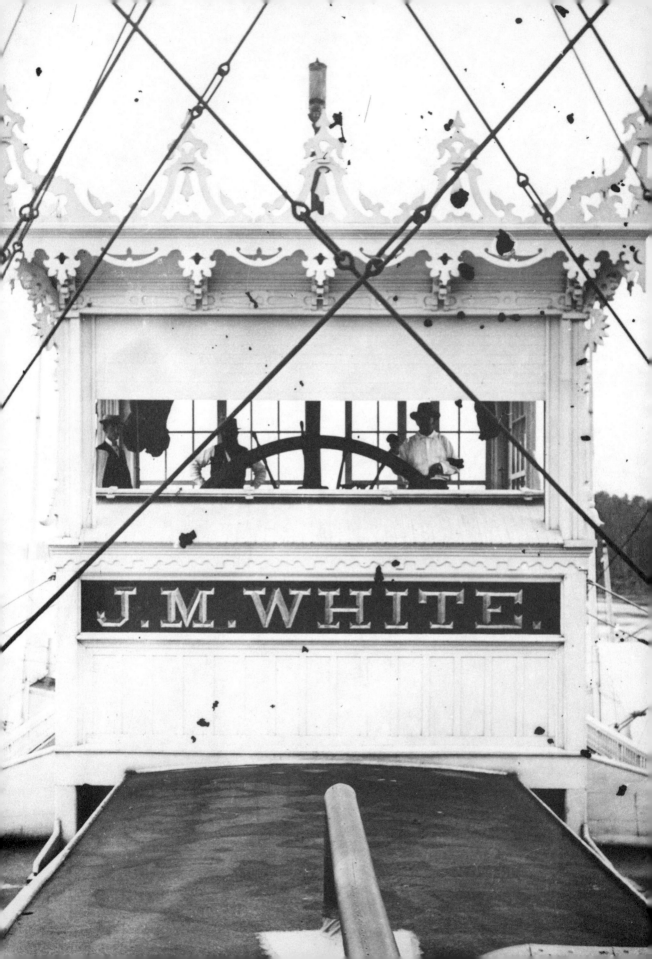

PILOT'S DELIGHT: A RIVER

COOKIN' BREAD BASKET

Limpa

⚓

Scandinavian communities along the upper riverbanks love limpa, a lightly spiced rye bread—the aroma of toasting limpa will make any morning brighter. To make superior, full-flavored whole grain breads, let the dough rise slowly in a not-too-warm place; use stone-ground, organic flours, available at natural food stores; and have a spray mister handy to spray your loaves to simulate the steamy interior of a professional baker's oven.

Makes two 8-inch round loaves

STARTER
½ cup water
½ teaspoon dry active yeast
½ cup unbleached all-purpose flour, preferably organic stone-ground
½ cup medium rye flour, preferably organic stone-ground

¾ cup water
¾ cup milk
1 teaspoon dry active yeast
Grated zest of 1 large orange
¼ cup unsulfured molasses

2 tablespoons unsalted butter, melted
1 teaspoon each dried anise, fennel, and caraway seeds, crushed
1 tablespoon salt
2 cups medium rye flour, preferably organic stone-ground
½ cup whole wheat flour, preferably organic stone-ground
2½ to 3 cups unbleached all-purpose flour, preferably organic stone-ground
Cornmeal, for dusting

1. *Make the Starter.* At least 2 hours before making the dough, in a small bowl, stir the water and yeast to dissolve the yeast. Stir in the flours to make a stiff dough. Cover with plastic wrap. Let stand at room temperature until the dough has a looser texture and is covered with tiny bubbles, at least 2 hours, preferably overnight but no longer than 10 hours.

2. *Make the Limpa.* In a medium saucepan, heat the water and milk until just tepid, not warm (90° to 100°F). Transfer to a large bowl and stir in the yeast. Add the starter, squeezing it through your fingers until broken up and partially dissolved. Stir in the orange zest, molasses, butter, anise, fennel, caraway seeds, and salt. Gradually stir in the rye and whole wheat flours. Add enough of the all-purpose flour to make a stiff, sticky dough. Turn the dough out onto a well-floured work surface and knead, adding more flour as needed, until smooth and elastic, at least 10 minutes. (The dough will be slightly tacky, which is a characteristic of rye doughs. Do not add too much unbleached flour.) Form the dough into a ball.

3. Lightly coat a large bowl with softened butter or vegetable shortening. Place the ball of dough in the bowl and turn to coat with butter. Cover with plastic wrap and let rise in a moderately warm (80° to 90°F) place, such as near a turned-on oven or clothes dryer. Let rise until about one and a half times its original volume, about 2 hours. (When the dough has risen enough, a finger inserted ½ inch into the dough will leave an impression.)

4. Cut the dough in half and form into two balls. Place them well apart on a large baking sheet that has been dusted with cornmeal. Cover with plastic wrap and let stand in a moderately warm (80° to 90°F) place until one and a half times their original volume, about 1 hour.

5. About 30 minutes before baking, place a baking stone (or a heavy large baking sheet) in the oven and preheat the oven to 450°F. With a serrated knife, slash an ⅛-inch-deep X into the top of each loaf. Place the baking sheet directly onto the preheated baking stone. Using a spray mister, quickly spray the loaves. Bake for 10 minutes, then lower the oven temperature to 375°F. Continue baking until the loaves sound hollow when tapped on the bottom with your knuckle, about 20 additional minutes. Cool them completely on a wire rack before serving.

Lagniappe: Rye flour comes in three shades: light, medium, and dark. Most supermarkets and natural food stores carry medium rye flour. Light flour is an acceptable substitute. Dark flour is very heavy and has lots of rye bran, so use less—for 2 cups of medium rye flour, substitute 1⅓ cups dark rye flour plus ⅔ cup all-purpose flour.

Sweet Potato Angel Biscuits

⚓

Angel biscuits have a bit of yeast in the dough, which makes them delightfully fluffy. I have given sweet potato biscuits, those Southern favorites, the "angel" treatment, and they are heavenly indeed, especially served warm for breakfast. The dough takes at least 3 hours to chill, so plan ahead.

Makes about 15 biscuits

1 pound sweet potatoes
    (Louisiana yams),
    unpeeled
1 teaspoon dry active yeast
2 tablespoons warm
    (100° to 110°F) water
2 cups all-purpose flour
3 tablespoons sugar,
    divided
1½ teaspoons baking
    powder

½ teaspoon baking soda
½ teaspoon salt
4 tablespoons unsalted
    butter, cut into ½-inch
    pieces, chilled
¼ cup vegetable
    shortening, chilled
½ cup buttermilk or ½ cup
    milk mixed with 1
    teaspoon cider vinegar
½ teaspoon ground
    cinnamon
Milk, for brushing

1. In a large saucepan of salted boiling water, cook the sweet potatoes until tender when pierced with the tip of a knife, 20 to 35 minutes, depending on size. Drain, rinse under cold water, and cool until tepid. Peel and mash until smooth. Measure and reserve 1 cup mashed sweet potatoes.

2. In a small bowl, dissolve the yeast in the warm water. In a medium bowl, whisk the flour, 2 tablespoons of the sugar, the baking powder, baking soda, and salt to combine. Cut in the butter and vegetable shortening with a pastry blender until crumbly. Add the dissolved yeast and mashed sweet potatoes and mix well. Stir in the buttermilk to make a soft, sticky dough. Cover with plastic wrap and refrigerate at least 3 hours, preferably overnight.

3. Preheat the oven to 400°F. Roll or pat out the dough to a ½-inch thickness on a lightly floured work surface. Cut out biscuits with a 2½-inch round cutter and place them about 1 inch apart on an ungreased baking sheet. Gather up the scraps, knead them again to combine, and reroll until all the dough is cut out. Combine the remaining 1 tablespoon sugar and cinnamon. Brush the tops of the biscuits with milk, then sprinkle with the cinnamon sugar. Bake until lightly browned, 12 to 15 minutes. Serve the biscuits warm.

Lagniappe: Boil the sweet potatoes with their skins on so they don't get soggy.

The choice of white flour (unbleached, bleached, or cake) in baked goods will make a big difference in the tenderness of the final product. Gluten is the protein in wheat that makes a dough strong. The amount of gluten in flour is in direct proportion to its protein content—the more protein, the more gluten. Unbleached flour has a high protein content and is best for kneaded bread doughs. Bleached flour loses some of its protein during processing, so it is a weaker dough that is best for pies, cookies, and general cooking purposes. Cake flour is an even more delicate flour that makes superior cakes. Where it is important in a recipe, I have stated what kind of flour to use.

❧❧

The term cotton pickin'
comes from the days of
river travel when
passengers shared deck
space with bales of cotton.
It wasn't long before the
travelers found their
clothes covered with tufts
of the white stuff, which
had to be painstakingly
removed by hand.

❧❧

Grandma Dunbar's Refrigerator Potato Dough Rolls

⚓

My dear friend Judith Dunbar Hines has shared many of her Missouri recipes with me. Her grandmother had a delicious habit of taking supper's leftover mashed potatoes and turning them into a dough to use for the dozens of rolls she prepared for the hungry farmhands. This dough keeps in the refrigerator for at least 3 days, so depending on your baking habits, you may want to make a double batch and do what Grandma Dunbar did—turn it into coffee cake (page 130) or potato bread (recipe follows) as well.

Makes about two dozen 3-inch rolls

1½ teaspoons dry yeast
½ teaspoon plus ¼ cup sugar, divided
¼ cup warm (100° to 110°F) water
1 cup milk
½ cup mashed potatoes (either plain or leftover seasoned)

¼ cup vegetable oil
1 large egg
2 teaspoons salt
Approximately 3½ cups unbleached all-purpose flour
1 tablespoon unsalted butter, melted, for brushing

1. At least one day before making the rolls, in a small bowl, dissolve the yeast with the ½ teaspoon sugar in the warm water. Let stand until foamy, about 5 minutes.

2. In a large bowl, combine the milk, mashed potatoes, yeast mixture, oil, remaining ¼ cup sugar, egg, and salt. Beat in 2 cups of the flour to make a stiff batter, then gradually beat in enough of the remaining flour to make a soft dough.

3. Turn out the dough onto a well-floured surface. Knead, adding more flour if necessary to keep the dough from sticking to the surface, until smooth and elastic, about 10 minutes. Form into a ball. Place in a lightly buttered large bowl and turn to coat the surface of the dough. Cover tightly with plastic wrap and refrigerate overnight, or up to 3 days.

4. When you are ready to bake, lightly butter two 9-inch cake pans. Form the dough into about twenty-four 2-inch balls. Arrange the balls in the prepared pans without touching each other. Cover the pans with plastic wrap. Place in a warm spot and let rise until the dough has almost doubled in bulk, about 90 minutes.

5. Preheat the oven to 375°F. Gently brush tops of the rolls with the melted butter. Bake until the rolls are golden brown, 18 to 20 minutes.

Lagniappe: You can also sprinkle the tops of the brushed rolls with sesame or poppy seeds before baking.

POTATO BREAD

To make potato bread, make the dough through Step 3. Divide the dough into 2 balls and knead each briefly. Form each ball into a loaf and press each evenly into a lightly buttered 8 × 4-inch loaf pan. Cover with plastic wrap and let stand in a warm (90°F) place until the dough has almost doubled in bulk and just reached the tops of the pans, about 2 hours. Preheat the oven to 375°F. Brush the tops with the melted butter and bake until the loaves are golden brown, about 30 minutes. The loaves are done when they sound hollow when tapped with a knuckle.

America's flour industry is centered in Minneapolis. The Falls of St. Anthony on the Mississippi attracted flour mills which processed wheat for the state's hungry loggers. Soon after his arrival in Minnesota in 1869, Charles Pillsbury took over a run-down mill on the falls and by 1887 became the world's largest flour miller. Pillsbury now also owns Green Giant (also a Minnesota success story), among its many other interests.

Grandma Dunbar's Sugar-Crust Coffee Cake

⚓

Once you have Grandma Dunbar's dough chilled in the refrigerator (made up through Step 3), you can easily whip this up when company comes calling.

Makes one 8-inch coffee cake, 6 servings

½ batch Grandma Dunbar's
   Refrigerator Potato
   Dough Rolls (page 128)
⅓ cup sugar

½ teaspoon ground
   cinnamon
1 tablespoon unsalted
   butter, melted

1. Lightly butter an 8-inch round cake pan. Pat the dough into a 6-inch-wide disk and place in the prepared pan. Cover with plastic wrap and let stand in a warm (90°F) place until almost doubled in bulk, about 1 hour 15 minutes.

2. Preheat the oven to 375°F. Mix the sugar and cinnamon together. Brush the top of the dough with the melted butter and sprinkle it evenly with the cinnamon sugar. Bake until golden brown and a toothpick inserted in the center comes out clean, 20 to 25 minutes. Let stand 5 minutes. Remove from the pan and transfer to a wire cake rack to cool for 15 minutes. Serve warm, cut lengthwise into thick slices, with softened butter for spreading if desired.

Sticky Raisin Swirl Bread

⚓

Sticky buns are served in bread baskets up and down the river. This tall, glorious loaf of raisin cinnamon buns is certainly their most dramatic incarnation. It's topped off with a baked-on caramel glaze, and the buns can be pulled apart easily for serving.

Makes one 10-inch loaf, about 12 servings

- **1 package (scant 2½ teaspoons) dry active yeast**
- **½ teaspoon plus ½ cup sugar, divided**
- **¼ cup warm (100° to 110°F) water**
- **1½ cups milk**
- **3 large eggs, beaten**
- **⅓ cup vegetable shortening, melted**
- **1 teaspoon salt**
- **Approximately 5 to 6 cups unbleached all-purpose flour**
- **¾ cup raisins**
- **½ teaspoon ground cinnamon**
- **10 tablespoons (5 ounces) unsalted butter, melted and divided**
- **½ cup packed light brown sugar**

1. In a small bowl, dissolve the yeast and the ½ teaspoon of sugar in the water and let stand until creamy, about 5 minutes. Stir to dissolve. In a large bowl, mix the milk, eggs, melted shortening, ¼ cup of the sugar, and salt. Stir in the dissolved yeast. Gradually stir in enough flour to make a stiff, soft, and sticky dough. Turn the dough out onto a well-floured work surface. Using well-floured hands, knead it, gradually working in enough flour to make a smooth, supple, and elastic dough, about 8 minutes. Form the dough into a ball.

2. Lightly coat a large bowl with softened butter or vegetable shortening. Place the dough in the bowl and turn to coat it with butter. Cover with plastic wrap. Place in a warm draft-free place and let rise until doubled in bulk, about 1½ hours.

3. Turn the dough onto a lightly floured work surface and knead briefly. Cover with plastic wrap and let rest for 10 minutes. Combine the raisins, remaining ¼ cup sugar, and cinnamon in a small bowl. On a lightly floured work surface, using a floured rolling pin, roll the dough out into a 10 × 15-inch rectangle. Brush the dough with 2 tablespoons of the melted butter. Sprinkle the raisin mixture over the surface of the dough. Starting with a long edge, roll up the dough jelly-roll fashion and cut crosswise into ¾-inch-wide slices.

4. Stir the brown sugar and the remaining 8 tablespoons of melted butter in a medium bowl until well combined. Coat a one-piece 10-inch tube pan (*without* a removable insert) or a Bundt pan with softened butter or vegetable shortening. Pour about one third of the glaze into the pan. Arrange the dough slices, standing upright and fitting closely, in the bottom of the pan. Drizzle the remaining glaze over the slices. Cover with plastic wrap and let stand in a warm place until almost doubled in bulk, about 1 hour. (When the dough has risen enough, a finger inserted ½ inch into the dough will leave an impression.)

5. Preheat the oven to 350°F. Bake for 30 minutes, then cover loosely with foil. Continue baking until the loaf sounds hollow when tapped with your knuckles, about 15 minutes. Carefully unmold the loaf onto a wire cake rack (if some of the raisins slide down the sides, use the tip of a knife to stick them on top). Let cool for 10 minutes. Serve the loaf warm or at room temperature, pulling the slices apart with your fingers.

Lagniappe: It's best to use solid fats, like shortening or butter, to coat the inside of the rising bowl. Liquid oil will be soaked up by the dough.

When the Austrian baker Charles Fleischmann was visiting Cincinnati in the 1860s, he was surprised at the low quality of American baked goods. After collecting European yeast samples, he returned to Ohio to formulate the first standarized compressed yeast. Fleischmann's yeast debuted in 1868, revolutionizing American baking. Two years later, Fleischmann and his partners formed The Fleischmann Distilling Company, providing America with its first gin.

When railroads triumphed in controlling the nation's transportation and cargo systems, the archaic steamboats slowly vanished. Ice, flood, accidents, and neglect claimed most boats, and some were dismantled, their parts put to other uses. There are only six remaining: The Belle of Louisville, *the* Julia Belle Swain, *the* Natchez, *and the Delta Queen Steamboat Co.'s* Delta Queen, Mississippi Queen, *and* American Queen. *Only the* Queens *offer staterooms for overnight travelers, making them the last survivors of the Golden Age of Steamboat Travel.*

Cheddar-Garlic-Grits
Spoon Bread

⚓

This creamy gussied-up version of cheesy grits is so tender it must be spooned out of the baking dish. You can spice it up by adding a fresh hot chile pepper, seeded and chopped, to the batter.

Makes 6 servings

½ cup yellow cornmeal
½ cup old-fashioned grits
   (not instant)
½ cup all-purpose flour
1 tablespoon sugar
1 teaspoon baking soda
1 teaspoon salt
1 cup buttermilk or 1 cup
   milk mixed with 1
   teaspoon cider vinegar

2 large eggs, beaten
1½ cups milk, divided
1 cup (4 ounces) shredded
   sharp Cheddar cheese
1 cup fresh or defrosted
   frozen corn kernels
1 garlic clove, minced
2 tablespoons unsalted
   butter, cut into small
   pieces

1. Preheat the oven to 400°F. In a large bowl, whisk the cornmeal, grits, flour, sugar, baking soda, and salt to combine. Stir in the buttermilk and eggs. Add 1 cup of the milk, the cheese, corn, and garlic and stir just to combine. Do not overmix.

2. Place the butter in a 10-inch round cake pan or cast-iron frying pan. Place in the oven and bake just until the butter melts, about 3 minutes. Tilt the pan to coat the bottom and sides with butter. Pour the batter into the pan and sprinkle the remaining ½ cup of milk over the top.

3. Return to the oven and bake until golden brown and a toothpick inserted 2 inches from the edge of the pan comes out clean and the center is barely set, about 25 minutes. Let stand 5 minutes. Serve the spoon bread warm.

Lagniappe: Turn this into a crab spoon bread casserole by spreading 8 ounces of crabmeat on the bottom of the hot pan before pouring in the batter.

Feather-Light Hush Puppies

⚓

Hush puppies, a cross between corn bread and fritters, were supposedly devised as a snack to quiet noisy (and hungry) hounds. Frankly, I have had hush puppies I haven't loved, but this is an exemplary recipe from *Kwanzaa: An African-American Celebration of Culture and Cooking* by Eric Copage (Morrow, 1991). They're crispy on the outside and creamy within—much too good to be given to dogs.

Makes about 3¹/₂ dozen hush puppies

Vegetable oil, for deep-frying

2 cups yellow cornmeal, preferably stone-ground

1 cup all-purpose flour

1 tablespoon baking powder

¹/₂ teaspoon baking soda

1 teaspoon salt

¹/₄ teaspoon ground hot red pepper, such as cayenne

1¹/₃ cups buttermilk or 1¹/₃ cups milk mixed with 1¹/₂ teaspoons cider vinegar

2 large eggs, well beaten

1 medium onion, minced

¹/₄ cup minced red bell pepper

1. Preheat the oven to 200°F. In a large deep skillet, heat enough oil to reach halfway up the sides until very hot but not smoking. (An electric skillet works perfectly for this.) A deep-fry thermometer will read 375°F. Be sure the oil is at the right temperature before making the batter.

2. In a medium bowl, whisk together the cornmeal, flour, baking powder, baking soda, salt, and hot red pepper. Make a well in the center of this mixture and pour the buttermilk and eggs into the well. Stir to make a stiff batter. Stir in the onion and red bell pepper.

3. Working in batches without crowding, drop the batter by heaping tablespoonfuls into the hot oil. Cook, turning each once, until both sides are golden brown, about 5 minutes. Using a slotted spoon, transfer the hush puppies to a paper towel–lined baking sheet to drain. Keep the cooked hush puppies warm in the oven while cooking the rest. Serve immediately.

Old-Fashioned Bacon Snip Corn Bread

⚓

Here's a somewhat crumbly corn bread that many folks prefer to more cakelike versions, as it does an even better job of soaking up gravy and butter. Sugar is a rather recent addition to corn bread (and one that many Southern cooks abhor), and it should be used in small quantities to complement, and not overwhelm, the cornmeal. This is the corn bread to use for making dressing, in which case you may choose to leave out the sugar altogether. This recipe makes the 10 cups of coarsely crumbled crumbs for Crab and Sausage Dressing on page 140 and can be halved easily.

Makes 12 to 16 servings, or 10 cups coarsely crumbled crumbs

6 ounces sliced bacon, cut into 1-inch pieces	1 teaspoon salt
2 cups all-purpose flour	2 cups milk
2 cups yellow cornmeal, preferably stone-ground	2 large eggs
2 tablespoons sugar (optional)	¼ cup bacon drippings
4 teaspoons baking soda	4 tablespoons (½ stick) unsalted butter, melted, plus more if needed
	1 cup fresh or defrosted frozen corn kernels

1. Preheat the oven to 375°F. Lightly butter a 13 × 9-inch baking pan.

2. In a medium skillet, cook the bacon over medium-high heat, stirring often, until crisp and browned, about 5 minutes. With a slotted spoon, transfer the bacon to paper towels to drain, reserving the bacon drippings. Measure out the bacon drippings, adding melted butter if necessary to make ¼ cup; set aside.

3. In a large bowl, whisk together the flour, cornmeal, sugar (optional), baking soda, and salt. Make a well in the center and add the milk, eggs, bacon drippings, and melted butter. Whisk just until smooth. Gently stir in the bacon and corn; do not overmix. Scrape into the prepared pan and smooth the top.

4. Bake until a toothpick inserted in the center comes out clean, 25 to 30 minutes. Serve warm or at room temperature.

Lagniappes: If you wish, use turkey bacon instead of pork bacon, and substitute ¼ cup vegetable oil for the bacon drippings.

For an 8-inch square corn bread, divide all the ingredients in half and bake for 20 to 25 minutes.

Corn bread recipes often call for being baked in a cast-iron skillet. As iron-made goods were very hard to come by in rural areas, settlers usually owned only three utensils for all their cooking needs—a footed skillet (called a spider), a pot similar to our Dutch oven, and sometimes a grid skillet for stove-top grilling.

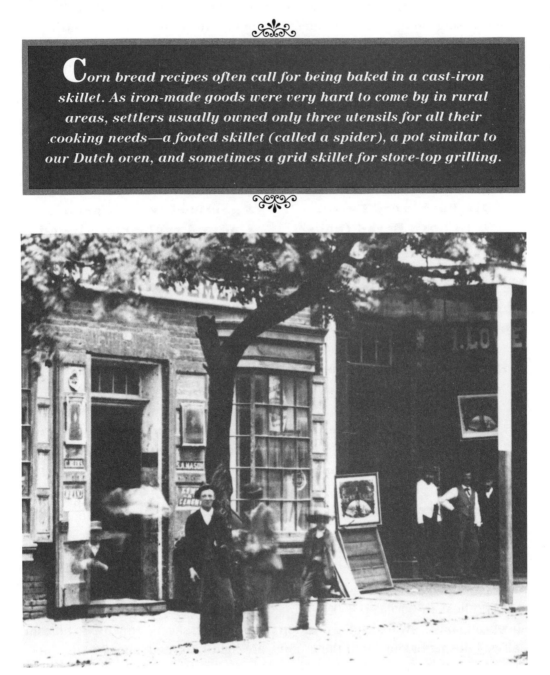

Crab and Sausage Dressing

⚓

Dressing and stuffing are really the same thing, the location of the kitchen deciding which it's called (it's *dressing* south of the Mason-Dixon line and *stuffing* north of it). You may choose the traditional route of stuffing the bird with dressing, but the extra poundage throws off the roasting time, contributes to the "dry white meat" problem, and can cause bacterial growth. I prefer to stuff my bird with a vegetable stuffing that flavors the meat and juices and bake my dressing separately (see page 50). If possible, make the corn bread a day or so ahead and let it stand out at room temperature to get stale before toasting.

Makes 12 to 16 servings

10 cups coarsely crumbled Old-Fashioned Bacon Snip Corn Bread (page 138), made without bacon, using ¼ cup melted butter instead of bacon drippings

8 tablespoons (1 stick) unsalted butter

12 ounces andouille or kielbasa sausage, cut into ½-inch pieces

1 large onion, chopped

2 medium celery ribs with leaves, chopped into ½-inch pieces

1 large sweet red bell pepper, seeded and chopped into ½-inch pieces

4 scallions, chopped

2 garlic cloves, minced

1 pound crabmeat, picked over for cartilage

⅓ cup chopped fresh parsley

2 tablespoons Bayou Seasoning (page 46)

1 tablespoon Worcestershire sauce

1 teaspoon salt

1 cup homemade turkey stock or canned chicken broth, plus additional if needed

½ cup half-and-half or light cream

1. Preheat the oven to 350°F. Spread the corn bread on two large baking sheets and bake, switching the position of the baking sheets from top to bottom halfway during baking, until the crumbs are lightly toasted, about 20 minutes. Transfer them to a large bowl.

2. In a large skillet, heat the butter over medium heat. Add the sausage, onion, celery, red bell pepper, scallions, and garlic and cook, stirring often, until the vegetables are softened, about 10 minutes. Stir in the crabmeat, parsley, Bayou Seasoning, Worcestershire sauce, and salt. Add to the toasted corn bread and mix well. Stir in the turkey stock and half-and half, adding additional stock if needed to moisten. Transfer to a buttered 15 × 10-inch baking dish and cover with aluminum foil. (The dressing can be prepared up to 6 hours ahead, covered and refrigerated. If you are stuffing the bird with the dressing, stuff it and bake immediately. Always stuff a turkey just before roasting, never the night before, even if it is refrigerated.)

3. Bake the dressing for 20 minutes. Remove the foil and continue baking until heated through and the top is lightly browned, about 20 additional minutes. Serve the dressing immediately.

On June 30, 1870, one of the most publicized media events of the day began: the race from New Orleans to St. Louis between the steamboats Rob't E. Lee *and* Natchez. *The* Rob't E. Lee *(nicknamed Hoppin' Bob) won with a finish time of 3 days, 18 hours, and 13 minutes. It was probably the biggest event to occur on the Mississippi up to that time, and millions of dollars in bets changed hands on both sides of the Atlantic.*

Pain Perdu Sandwiches
with Orange Syrup

⚓

In French, *pain perdu* means "lost bread," unwanted stale slices that find new life when soaked in an egg batter and sautéed until golden brown. This was the prototype for French toast. I like to sandwich fillings into my pain perdu, using smoked turkey or ham, or even raspberry preserves or grated chocolate for sweet-tooth mornings. Maple syrup is not much appreciated in the South, and honey or cane syrup is used most often as the topping—you can simply use what you have on hand.

Makes 4 sandwiches

1 cup half-and-half, light cream, or milk
2 large eggs
4 tablespoons Grand Marnier or defrosted frozen orange juice concentrate, divided
8 slices firm-textured white bread, French bread, or challah

8 slices smoked turkey
1 tablespoon unsalted butter
1 tablespoon vegetable oil
¾ cup honey, cane syrup, or maple syrup

1. In a medium bowl, beat the half-and-half, eggs, and 2 tablespoons of the Grand Marnier until well combined. Make 4 sandwiches, using 2 slices of bread and smoked turkey for each. (The batter, covered, and the sandwiches, wrapped in plastic wrap, can be made up to 8 hours ahead and refrigerated until ready to cook.)

2. Preheat the oven to 200°F. In a large skillet, heat the butter and oil over medium heat. One at a time, dip the sandwiches in the batter and let the excess batter drip off. Place the sandwiches in batches if necessary in the skillet and cook until the underside is golden brown, about 3 minutes. (Adjust the heat if necessary so the sandwiches don't burn.) Turn them and cook until the other side is golden brown, another 3 minutes. Keep the sandwiches warm in the oven.

3. Meanwhile, in a small saucepan, heat the honey until warm. Off the heat, stir in the remaining 2 tablespoons of Grand Marnier, and pour into a warmed sauceboat. Serve immediately with the warm sandwiches.

Even though maple syrup is native to New England, perhaps the best known of all maple syrups, Log Cabin Syrup, originated in St. Paul, Minnesota. In the late 1880s, a grocer first blended expensive maple syrup with less costly corn syrup to create a reasonably priced product.

WEIGHING ANCHOR:

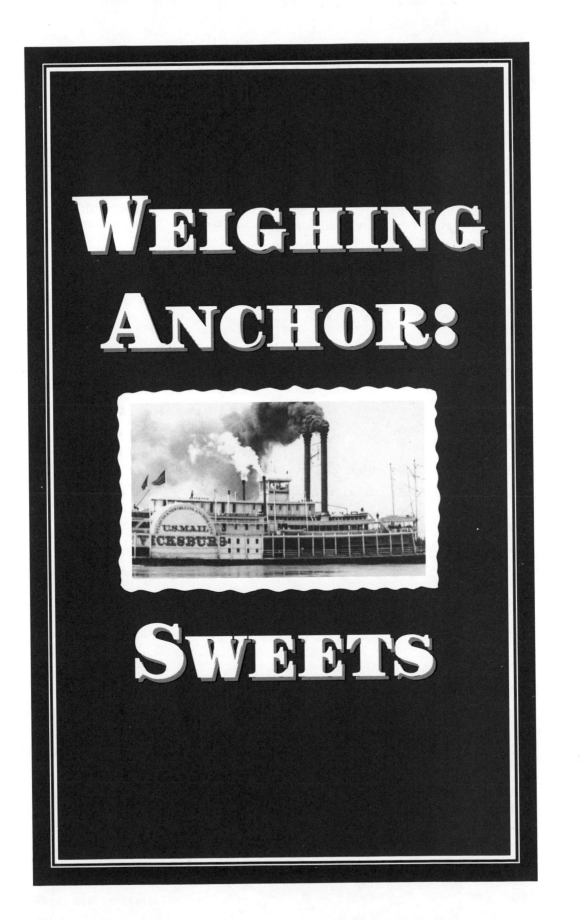

SWEETS

Blackberry-Caramel
Bread Pudding

⚓

Juicy blackberries grow profusely up and down the river, and each summer, savvy cooks are found foraging in the thickets to fill up buckets with the luscious fruit. Bread pudding is a New Orleans favorite that hardly needs any improving, but the caramel and blackberry embellishments gild the lily beautifully.

Makes 6 to 8 servings

6 cups half-and-half
8 tablespoons (1 stick) unsalted butter, cut into pieces
2 cups sugar
¼ cup water
6 large eggs, at room temperature

1½ teaspoons vanilla extract
8 cups (1-inch cubes) day-old French or Italian bread, crusts trimmed
1 pint fresh blackberries

1. In a medium saucepan, heat the half-and-half and butter over medium heat, stirring often to melt the butter. Do not let the mixture boil over. Set aside.

2. In a large saucepan, stir the sugar and water over high heat until boiling. Stop stirring and boil, washing down any sugar crystals that form on the sides of the pan with a wet pastry brush, until the syrup turns golden brown, about 5 minutes. Remove from the heat. Being careful not to let the mixture boil over, carefully whisk the hot milk into the caramel. Return the milk mixture to the stove. Cook over low heat, whisking to completely dissolve the caramel. Remove from the heat and cool for 10 minutes.

3. In a very large bowl, whisk the eggs and vanilla. Gradually whisk in the hot milk mixture. Add the bread cubes and stir well. Let stand 15 minutes, stirring often so the bread cubes soak up the liquids evenly.

4. Preheat the oven to 325°F. Spread the blackberries in the bottom of a lightly buttered 13 × 9-inch baking dish. Pour in the bread mixture and place the baking dish into a larger baking pan, arranging the bread cubes so the berries are submerged. Place in the oven and add enough hot water to come ½ inch up the sides of the smaller dish. Bake until a knife inserted in the center of the pudding comes out clean, about 1 hour. Cool slightly, then serve warm or at room temperature.

Lagniappe: If the bread cubes aren't stale, spread them on baking sheets and bake in a preheated 350°F oven until slightly dried out, about 10 minutes.

The Joy of Cooking, *one of the best-selling cookbooks ever, was originally a small, privately published book by St. Louis resident Irma Rombauer. It took years of perseverance before she convinced a publisher to print an edition of 7,000 copies. By the mid-1980s the book had sold over 10 million copies.*

Banana, Raspberry, and Peach Cookie Trifle

⚓

Trifle, a larger-than-average dessert fit for feeding a crowd, is anything but inconsequential. Using vanilla wafers (instead of cake) turns trifle into a nostalgic dessert reminiscent of that famous Southern treat, banana-wafer pudding. Few Southern cooks fuss with making their own vanilla sauce, and you can mix 2 boxes of instant vanilla pudding with 4 cups of milk to substitute for the ingredients in Step 2.

Makes 10 to 12 servings

2 pounds ripe fresh peaches, peeled, pitted, and sliced

1 tablespoon plus 1 cup sugar, divided

1 tablespoon peach-flavored schnapps (optional)

¼ cup all-purpose flour

6 large egg yolks

3 cups milk, heated to scalding

2½ teaspoons vanilla extract, divided

2 medium ripe bananas, sliced

2 pints fresh raspberries

⅓ cup bourbon or apple cider

1 11-ounce box vanilla wafers

1 cup heavy cream

1 tablespoon confectioners' sugar

1. In a medium bowl, gently mix the peaches, the 1 tablespoon of sugar, and the peach schnapps. Cover and refrigerate at least 2 hours, or overnight.

2. In a medium heavy-bottomed saucepan, whisk together the remaining 1 cup of sugar, flour, and egg yolks. Gradually whisk in the milk. Stirring constantly, bring to a simmer over medium-low heat, then cook for 2 minutes. Remove from the heat and whisk in 2 teaspoons of the vanilla. Transfer to a medium bowl and cover with a piece of plastic wrap pressed directly onto the surface of the sauce. Using the tip of a sharp knife, pierce holes in the plastic wrap to release steam. Cool to room temperature.

3. Just before making the trifle, gently stir the bananas, raspberries, and bourbon into the peaches. Layer one third of the wafers on the bottom of a 3-quart trifle bowl. Spoon in one third of the fruit, then one third of the vanilla sauce. Repeat the layering procedure twice, using the remaining wafers, fruit, and vanilla sauce. Cover with plastic wrap and refrigerate at least 2 hours, or overnight.

4. In a chilled medium bowl, beat the heavy cream and confectioners' sugar just until stiff peaks form. Swirl the whipped cream on top of the trifle and serve chilled.

*P**eaches are an important Arkansas crop, the original cuttings having been planted by the Cherokees, who brought them from their homes farther south. (The Spaniards originally brought the trees from Europe.) Today's Arkansas peaches are the hardy Elberta variety, introduced in the late 1890s.***

Peanut Butter Cake with Milk Chocolate–Peanut Frosting

⚓

America loves cake, peanuts, and chocolate—and the combination of the three in this luscious old-fashioned layer cake will transport dessert lovers.

Makes one 9-inch cake, 6 to 8 servings

PEANUT BUTTER CAKE
2 cups cake flour (not self-rising)
1 tablespoon baking powder
⅛ teaspoon salt
8 tablespoons (1 stick) unsalted butter, at room temperature
½ cup chunky peanut butter

1 cup sugar
2 large eggs, at room temperature
1 teaspoon vanilla extract
1 cup milk

MILK CHOCOLATE–PEANUT FROSTING
12 ounces milk chocolate, coarsely chopped
¾ cup chunky peanut butter
½ cup confectioners' sugar

1. *Make the Cake.* Position a rack in the center of the oven and preheat the oven to 350°F. Lightly butter the bottom of two 9-inch cake pans. Line the bottoms of the pans with rounds of waxed paper. Dust the insides of the pans with flour and tap out the excess. Sift together the flour, baking powder, and salt through a sieve onto a piece of waxed paper and set aside.

2. In a large bowl, using a hand-held electric mixer on high speed, beat the butter and peanut butter until smooth, about 1 minute. Add the sugar and continue beating until light in texture and color, about 3 minutes. One at a time, beat in the eggs, then the vanilla. Alternately in thirds, with the mixer on low speed, add the flour mixture and the milk, scraping the sides of the bowl with a rubber spatula. Scrape the batter into the prepared pans and smooth the tops.

3. Bake until the tops of the layers spring back when pressed lightly in the center, 25 to 30 minutes. Transfer the pans to a wire cake rack and cool for 10 minutes. Run a sharp knife around the edges of the cakes to loosen and invert them onto a wire cake rack. Carefully peel off the waxed paper, turn the layers right side up, and cool completely. (The cake layers can be prepared up to 1 day ahead, wrapped tightly in plastic wrap and stored at room temperature, or frozen for up to 1 month.)

4. *Make the Frosting.* In the top of a double boiler set over hot, not simmering, water, melt the milk chocolate. Remove the top of the double boiler from the heat and let stand until the chocolate is cool but still liquid, about 10 minutes.

5. In a medium bowl, using a hand-held electric mixer on medium speed, beat the cooled chocolate and peanut butter until smooth. Gradually beat in the confectioners' sugar and beat until light and fluffy, about 1 minute.

6. To assemble the cake, place one cake layer upside down on a serving platter. Frost the top of the layer with some of the frosting. Place the second layer, right side up, on top. Frost the top and sides of the cake with the remaining frosting. (The finished cake can be prepared up to 1 day ahead, loosely covered with plastic wrap and stored at room temperature. If refrigerated, let the cake come to room temperature before serving.)

Peanuts play a large part in the agricultural history of the river. They are believed to have originated in Brazil and were found growing in Haiti by Columbus. The Spanish and Portuguese brought them back to Europe, and they also became a West African crop. Even though they were grown sporadically in the South during the slave era, it wasn't until the 1890s that peanuts became a staple crop. Southern farms were desperately searching for a product to replace cotton, which had been destroyed by boll weevils. George Washington Carver promoted the peanut's nutritive value and appealing taste, and the Southern farmers were saved from disaster.

Steamboating
increasingly faced fierce
competition from the
railroads. But boats like
the Greenland attracted
loyal passengers by
offering the kind of
unparalleled luxury that
the railroad had not yet
achieved. And steamboats
were not just for cruising
or transporting cotton.
Many, like the Betty Ann,
were built to transport
mail and freight, a
practice that continued
until about 1940.

Berry-Apple Cobbler

⚓

Apple orchards and berry patches are found side by side along the riverbanks, but it never occurred to me to combine the two fruits in a dessert. One late-summer afternoon, though, I didn't have enough of either to make a single-flavor cobbler, so I mixed them together and got a winning dessert with chunks of tart apples in a sweet berry sauce, topped with a tender crust.

Makes 6 to 8 servings

7 medium Granny Smith apples, peeled, cored, and cut into ½-inch wedges
1 pint fresh blackberries
1 pint fresh raspberries
¾ cup packed light brown sugar
⅓ cup plus 1½ cups all-purpose flour, divided
2 tablespoons lemon juice
¾ teaspoon ground cinnamon

8 tablespoons (1 stick) unsalted butter, cut into small pieces, divided
½ cup granulated sugar
¼ cup yellow cornmeal, preferably stone-ground
1 tablespoon baking powder
½ teaspoon salt
¾ cup half-and-half
Sweetened whipped cream or vanilla ice cream

1. Preheat the oven to 375°F. In a large bowl, place the apples, berries, brown sugar, the ⅓ cup of flour, lemon juice, and cinnamon. Toss gently, then spread the fruit into the bottom of a 13 × 9-inch baking dish. Dot the top of the fruit with 2 tablespoons of the butter.

2. In a medium bowl, stir together the remaining 1½ cups of flour, sugar, cornmeal, baking powder, and salt. Using a pastry blender or two knives, cut in the remaining 6 tablespoons of butter until the mixture resembles coarse meal. Tossing with a fork, gradually sprinkle in the half-and-half, mixing just until a soft dough is formed.

3. Drop large spoonfuls of dough randomly over the top of the fruit. Bake until the fruit is tender and bubbling and a toothpick inserted into the topping comes out clean, about 55 minutes. If the top browns too quickly, cover loosely with a piece of foil. Serve warm with whipped cream or ice cream.

Minnesota's Red River Valley boasts that it is "America's sugar bowl," home to over 16,500 sugar beet growers.

"A steamboat is as beautiful as a wedding cake, but without the complications."
Mark Twain

Gingerbread Stout Cake

⚓

Beer reigns as the favorite beverage in the river states. British and German bakers have long loved gingerbread cakes, and the addition of rich, malty, caramel-scented stout makes this recipe extraordinary, especially when served warm.

Makes one 12-inch cake, 8 to 12 servings

2½ cups all-purpose flour
2 teaspoons ground ginger
2 teaspoons ground cinnamon
2 teaspoons baking soda
½ teaspoon ground cloves
½ teaspoon salt
1 cup (2 sticks) unsalted butter, at room temperature

1¼ cups packed light brown sugar
2 large eggs, at room temperature
1 cup unsulfured molasses
¾ cup stout, flat, at room temperature
Confectioners' sugar, for garnish
Sweetened whipped cream (optional)

1. Preheat the oven to 350°F. Butter and flour the inside of a 12-cup fluted cake pan, tapping out the excess flour. Sift together the flour, ginger, cinnamon, baking soda, cloves, and salt through a sieve onto a piece of waxed paper.

2. In a large bowl, with a hand-held electric mixer on high speed, beat the butter and brown sugar until light in texture, about 1 minute. Beat in the eggs, one at a time, then beat in the molasses. Lower the mixer to medium speed and beat in the flour, one third at a time, scraping down the sides of the bowl often. Beat in the stout.

3. Pour the batter into the prepared pan, smoothing the top with a rubber scraper. Bake until a toothpick inserted in the center comes out clean, 50 to 60 minutes. Cool the cake on a wire rack for 10 minutes before unmolding onto a wire cake rack. Dust with confectioners' sugar. Serve warm or completely cooled, with whipped cream if desired.

Upriver Deep-Dish Apple Pie with Cheese Crust

⚓

Cheese and apples are a happy combination, and possibly never happier than when mixed together in a homemade pie. You can make this with either extra-sharp Wisconsin Cheddar or with milder Gouda, preferably one of the hand-made versions from Minnesota.

Makes 8 servings

CHEESE CRUST
2 cups all-purpose flour
½ teaspoon salt
½ cup vegetable shortening, chilled and cut into small pieces
½ cup (2 ounces) shredded extra-sharp Cheddar or Gouda cheese
3 tablespoons unsalted butter, chilled and cut into ½-inch cubes
6 tablespoons ice water, approximately
1 teaspoon lemon juice

2 Granny Smith apples, peeled, cored, and cut into ½-inch-thick slices

2 McIntosh apples, peeled, cored, and cut into ½-inch-thick slices
2 Golden Delicious apples, peeled, cored, and cut into ½-inch-thick slices
¼ cup sugar
2 tablespoons all-purpose flour
¼ teaspoon ground cinnamon
½ cup (2 ounces) shredded extra-sharp Cheddar or Gouda cheese, divided
2 tablespoons unsalted butter, cut into small pieces
1 large egg yolk beaten with 1 tablespoon milk to make a glaze

1. *Make the Crust.* In a medium bowl, combine the flour and salt. Using a pastry blender or two knives, cut in the shortening, ½ cup shredded cheese, and butter until the mixture resembles coarse meal, with a few pieces of fat that are the size of small peas. In a small bowl, mix the ice water and lemon juice. Tossing the mixture with a fork, gradually sprinkle in the ice water until just moistened and the dough holds together when pinched between your thumb and forefinger. (You may have to add more ice water, 1 tablespoon at a time.) Gather up the dough and cut into two pieces in one-third and two-thirds proportions. Press each into a thick flat disk, wrap in waxed paper, and refrigerate until well chilled, at least 1 hour. (The dough can be prepared up to 2 days ahead, covered and refrigerated.)

2. Place a heavy baking sheet in the bottom third of the oven and preheat oven to 425°F. In a large bowl, toss together the apples, sugar, flour, and cinnamon until the apples are well coated and set aside. On a lightly floured work surface, using a lightly floured rolling pin, roll out the larger portion of dough into a 12-inch circle about ⅛ inch thick. Gently transfer the dough to a 9-inch pie pan. Sprinkle the bottom of the crust with 6 tablespoons of the cheese. Arrange the apple mixture in the pie crust and dot with the butter pieces. Roll out the smaller portion of dough into a 10-inch circle about ⅛ inch thick, and place over the apples. Press the edges of the crusts together to seal. Roll up the excess dough around the edges to form a thick rope and flute it. Cut a 2-inch slash in the top crust. Lightly brush the top of the pie with some of the egg glaze.

3. Place the pie on the heated baking sheet and bake for 10 minutes. Reduce the oven to 375°F and continue baking until crust is golden brown and the apples are barely tender when pierced through the slash in the crust with the tip of a sharp knife, about 30 additional minutes. Transfer the pie to a wire cake rack and sprinkle with the remaining 2 tablespoons of cheese. Cool and serve warm or at room temperature.

Lagniappe: Minnesota Gouda cheese is available by mail order from Baune's Minnesota Farmstead Cheese, Highway 169 North, Milaca, MN 56353 (612-983-6576).

The University of Minnesota, in order to maintain family farms and provide job opportunities in rural areas, established a cheese-making program in the late 1970s. With the help of Dutch cheese makers, the university dairy specialists developed a Gouda recipe, which was passed on to a small group of farmers. The farms all operate under the cooperative name Minnesota Farmstead Gouda.

Best-Ever Strawberry Shortcakes

⚓

Everyone has a recipe for strawberry shortcake, but I must immodestly boast that this version is world-class. The biscuits are tall, flaky, and buttery, their secret being homemade baking powder (a baking soda/cream of tartar combination) and a mixture of both cake and all-purpose flours. Be sure to make the berry filling far enough ahead of time for the berries to release their juices.

Makes 8 servings

BERRY FILLING
4 cups fresh berries
    (blackberries,
    raspberries, hulled and
    halved strawberries, or a
    combination)
⅓ cup sugar
1 tablespoon fresh lemon
    juice

SHORTCAKE
1 cup cake flour (not self-
    rising)
1 cup all-purpose flour
2 tablespoons sugar

2 teaspoons cream of tartar
1 teaspoon baking soda
½ teaspoon salt
8 tablespoons (1 stick)
    unsalted butter, chilled
    and cut into ¼-inch
    cubes
¾ cup half-and-half

ASSEMBLY
2 cups heavy cream
¼ cup confectioners' sugar
2 teaspoons vanilla extract
Berries, for garnish

1. *Make the Filling.* Set aside some of the prettiest berries for garnishing. In a large bowl, gently stir together the berries, sugar, and lemon juice to combine. Cover the bowl tightly with plastic wrap and refrigerate for at least 4 hours, or overnight, until the berries release their juices.

2. *Make the Shortcakes.* Position a rack in the center of the oven and preheat the oven to 400°F. Into a medium bowl, sift the the flours, sugar, cream of tartar, baking soda, and salt. Using a pastry blender or two knives, cut the butter into the flour mixture until the butter is the size of small peas. Add the half-and-half and stir until the mixture forms a soft dough. Knead the dough about 6 times in the bowl, until smooth. Do not overhandle the dough.

3. On a lightly floured work surface, using a lightly floured rolling pin, roll out the dough to a ¾-inch thickness. Using a 3½-inch biscuit cutter, or a glass with a 3½-inch diameter, cut out 5 shortcakes. Place the shortcakes on an ungreased baking sheet. Gather up the dough scraps and press them into a flat disk. Roll and cut out 3 more shortcakes and place them on the baking sheet. Bake for 12 to 15 minutes, or until the shortcakes are golden brown. Cool the shortcakes slightly on the baking sheet.

4. *Assemble the Shortcakes.* In a chilled large bowl, using a hand-held electric mixer on medium-high, beat the cream, confectioners' sugar, and vanilla until soft peaks form.

5. Using a serrated knife, slice each shortcake in half. Place the bottom halves on dessert plates. Spoon the berries and juice over the bottom halves. Top each with a large dollop of whipped cream. Place a shortcake top on the whipped cream and top with another large dollop of whipped cream. Garnish with the reserved berries. Serve immediately.

During the Midwest's pioneer days, "strawberry socials" were held in the community to help pick the strawberry crop. For their efforts, people were rewarded with a picnic lunch and, of course, strawberry shortcake.

Steamboating offered men a career full of adventure and independence. But there were a few women bold enough to try their hand at the wheel. Because they were so rare, the few women who did earn their pilot's and master's licenses were well known and well respected along the river. Whether man or woman, one trait ran true for any pilot: "the proper ambition of any muddle-headed steamboater is someday to have a bigger boat," according to one owner, Tom Greene.

Sweet Potato Pie with
Marshmallow Crown

⚓

Sweet potato pie is one of my favorite desserts, its sweet and spicy flavor particularly welcome during the winter holidays. But be warned: When the weather is humid, don't attempt the marshmallow crown—it could melt into a sticky mess. Instead, top the pie with sweetened whipped cream.

Makes 8 to 10 servings

CRUST
2 cups all-purpose flour
½ teaspoon salt
⅔ cup vegetable shortening, chilled and cut into small pieces
⅓ cup ice water, plus more if necessary

SWEET POTATO FILLING
2 medium (1 pound) sweet potatoes (Louisiana yams), scrubbed and unpeeled
4 tablespoons (½ stick) unsalted butter, at room temperature

½ cup sugar
3 large eggs, separated, at room temperature
½ cup evaporated milk
1 8¼-ounce can crushed pineapple in juice, drained, the juice reserved
1 tablespoon reserved pineapple juice
¾ teaspoon ground cinnamon
⅛ teaspoon grated nutmeg
1½ cups miniature marshmallows

1. *Make the Crust.* In a medium bowl, combine the flour and salt. Using a pastry blender or two knives, cut in the shortening until the mixture resembles coarse meal, with a few pieces of shortening the size of small peas. Tossing the mixture with a fork, gradually sprinkle in the ⅓ cup ice water, mixing with the fork, until just moistened and holds together when pinched between your thumb and forefinger. (You may have to add more ice water, 1 tablespoon at a time.) Gather up the dough into a thick flat disk, wrap it in waxed paper, and refrigerate for at least 1 hour, or up to 2 days.

2. Place a baking sheet on a rack in the bottom third of the oven and preheat the oven to 400°F. Roll out dough on a lightly floured work surface to a 14-inch circle about ⅛ inch thick. Carefully transfer the dough to a 10-inch deep-dish pie plate. Trim the dough to a 1-inch overhang. Fold over the excess dough into a thick rope and flute the edges. Prick the bottom of the dough with a fork. Cover the dough with plastic wrap and freeze for 30 minutes.

3. Line the inside of the pastry-filled pan with aluminum foil and weight the foil-lined dough with dried beans or rice. Place the pie shell on the preheated baking sheet. Bake until the dough is set, but not colored, about 10 minutes. Remove the foil and beans. Transfer to a wire cake rack and set aside. Keep the oven at 400°F.

4. *Make the Filling.* Meanwhile, in a large saucepan of lightly salted boiling water, cook the sweet potatoes until tender, about 30 minutes. Drain and rinse them under cold running water until cool enough to handle. Peel the sweet potatoes and place them in a large bowl. Add the butter and mash until smooth. Stir in the sugar, egg yolks, evaporated milk, crushed pineapple, reserved pineapple juice, cinnamon, and nutmeg. In a medium grease-free bowl, beat the egg whites just until soft peaks form. Fold into the sweet potato mixture and spread into the prepared shell.

5. Bake the pie for 10 minutes. Reduce the heat to 350°F and bake until a knife inserted in the center of the pie comes out clean, about 45 additional minutes. Remove from the oven and immediately arrange a single layer of marshmallows on top of the pie. Cool the pie completely on a wire cake rack. Serve the pie warm, chilled, or at room temperature.

Lagniappe: Freezing the dough-lined pan before baking helps reduce shrinkage.

A true sweet potato has a pale yellow flesh and is only mildly sweet. In the Caribbean it is called a batata, *from which we get our word for potato. The orange-fleshed sweet potato is called a Louisiana yam.*

Café Brûlot Chiffon Pie

⚓

Café Brûlot ("burnt coffee") is a flambéed, spiced, and brandy-spiked after-dinner beverage. Here the citrus-and-cinnamon-scented coffee is transformed into a luscious chiffon pie crowned with brandy-flavored cream and chocolate curls.

Makes 8 servings

CRUST
1½ cups all-purpose flour
½ teaspoon salt
⅓ cup vegetable
   shortening, chilled and
   cut into small pieces
2 tablespoons unsalted
   butter, chilled and cut
   into small pieces
¼ cup ice water, plus more
   if necessary

CHIFFON FILLING
1 envelope unflavored
   gelatin
2 tablespoons plus 1 cup
   water, divided
4 whole allspice berries
1 cinnamon stick

2 2-inch strips of lemon
   zest (remove with a
   vegetable peeler)
2 2-inch strips of orange
   zest (remove with a
   vegetable peeler)
½ cup sugar
1 tablespoon instant
   espresso coffee powder
3 tablespoons brandy,
   divided
1½ cups heavy cream,
   divided
3 large egg whites, at room
   temperature
1 tablespoon
   confectioners' sugar
Chocolate curls, for
   garnish (see Lagniappe)

1. *Make the Crust.* In a medium bowl, combine the flour and salt. Using a pastry blender or two knives, cut in the shortening and butter until the mixture resembles coarse meal, with a few pieces of shortening the size of small peas. Tossing the mixture with a fork, gradually sprinkle in the ¼ cup ice water, mixing with the fork, until just moistened and holds together when pinched between your thumb and forefinger. (You may have to add more ice water, 1 tablespoon at a time.) Gather up the dough into a thick flat disk, wrap in waxed paper, and refrigerate for at least 1 hour, or up to 2 days.

2. Preheat the oven to 375°F. On a lightly floured work surface, roll out the dough to a 12-inch circle about ⅛ inch thick. Carefully transfer the dough to a 9-inch pie pan. Fold over the excess dough into a thick rope and flute the edges. Prick the bottom of the dough with a fork. Line the inside of the pastry-filled pan with aluminum foil and weight the foil-lined dough with dry beans or rice. Freeze the pie shell for 30 minutes.

3. Bake until the dough is set, about 10 minutes. Remove the foil and beans and continue baking until the pie shell is golden brown, about 15 minutes longer. Cool completely on a wire cake rack.

4. *Make the Filling.* In a small bowl, sprinkle the gelatin over the 2 table-spoons of water and set aside to soften. In a medium saucepan, bring the remaining 1 cup water, the allspice, cinnamon, and lemon and orange zest to a simmer over low heat. Remove from the heat and whisk in the softened gelatin, sugar, and instant coffee until dissolved. Stir in 2 tablespoons of the brandy. Let stand for 5 minutes, then strain into a medium bowl, discarding the solids. Refrigerate the coffee mixture, stirring occasionally, until cold and thickened but not set, about 1 hour.

5. In a chilled small bowl, beat ½ cup of the heavy cream until just stiff. In a medium grease-free bowl, beat the egg whites just until soft peaks form. Using a rubber spatula, fold the cream and then egg whites into the thickened coffee mixture. Pour into the cooled pie shell. Cover loosely with plastic wrap and refrigerate until set, at least 2 hours.

6. In a chilled medium bowl, beat the remaining 1 cup heavy cream with the confectioners' sugar until stiff. Beat in the remaining 1 tablespoon brandy. Swirl the whipped cream over the top of the pie and garnish with the chocolate curls.

Lagniappe: To make chocolate curls, warm a 4-ounce chunk of chocolate in a microwave for 30 seconds at medium. (Just warm the chocolate slightly—don't let it melt. You may also warm the chocolate chunk underneath a desk lamp.) Using a vegetable peeler, make the curls by pressing down while peeling them off of the smoothest, widest edge of the chunk. The harder you press, the thicker the curls. Let the curls fall onto a waxed paper–lined plate and refrigerate until ready to use.

Derby Chocolate Pecan Pie

⚓

When Kentucky Derby time comes around, Louisville cooks outdo themselves in preparing sumptuous spreads. Since desserts are very popular, the array of sweets can be overwhelming. One of them, this chocolate pecan pie, is an easy-to-make favorite.

Makes one 9-inch pie

CRUST
1½ cups all-purpose flour
½ teaspoon salt
⅓ cup vegetable
 shortening, chilled and
 cut into pieces
2 tablespoons unsalted
 butter, chilled and cut
 into pieces
About ¼ cup ice water

⅓ cup sugar
3 tablespoons unsalted
 butter, melted
2 tablespoons bourbon
1 teaspoon vanilla extract
6 ounces (about 1½ cups)
 pecan halves, coarsely
 chopped
¾ cup semisweet chocolate
 chips

FILLING
3 large eggs
1 cup light corn syrup

1. *Make the Crust.* In a medium bowl, stir together the flour and salt. Using a pastry blender or two knives, cut in the shortening and butter until the mixture resembles coarse meal. Tossing with a fork, gradually sprinkle in the ice water, mixing until the dough is just moist enough to hold together when pinched between your thumb and forefinger. (You may need to add more ice water.) Gather the dough into a thick disk, wrap it in waxed paper, and chill for at least 1 hour, or overnight.

2. On a lightly floured work surface, roll out the pastry into a 12-inch circle about ⅛ inch thick. (If the dough cracks, it is too cold. Let it stand at room temperature for 5 minutes before proceeding.) Ease the dough into a 9-inch pie pan. Roll the excess dough over to form a rope, then crimp the dough decoratively.

3. *Make the Filling.* Position a rack in the bottom third of the oven. Place a baking sheet on the rack and preheat the oven to 350°F. In a medium bowl, whisk the eggs well. Whisk in the corn syrup, sugar, melted butter, bourbon, and vanilla. Stir in the pecans and chocolate chips. Pour the mixture into the prepared pie shell.

4. Place on the preheated baking sheet and bake until a knife inserted halfway between the center and the edge of the pie comes out clean, 50 to 60 minutes. Cool the pie completely on a wire rack. (The pie can be prepared up to 2 days ahead, covered with plastic wrap and stored at room temperature.)

Lagniappe: Baking on the preheated baking sheet, and in the bottom third of the oven, helps crisp the pie's bottom crust, which can get soggy from the pecan filling.

Peach Tart Ste. Genevieve

⚓

Ste. Genevieve, Missouri, is a reminder of the French Colonial days, which lasted until 1763, when France ceded its American holdings to Great Britain and Spain. This European-style, almond-scented tart looks lovely and is quite easy to make, for the dough isn't rolled out but pressed directly into the tart pan.

Makes 6 to 8 servings

7 fresh peaches (about 2 pounds), pitted, peeled, and cut into ½-inch slices

2 tablespoons cornstarch

½ cup sugar, divided

¼ cup sliced almonds

9 tablespoons (1 stick plus 1 tablespoon) unsalted butter, at room temperature, divided

1 large egg, divided

¼ teaspoon almond extract

1 cup all-purpose flour

1. Preheat the oven to 375°F. In a medium bowl, toss the peach slices with the cornstarch and ⅓ cup of the sugar and set aside.

2. In a food processor fitted with a metal blade, process the almonds with 1 tablespoon of the sugar until very fine. With a hand-held electric mixer on high speed, mix the remaining 2 tablespoons sugar with 8 tablespoons of the butter until it is light in color and fluffy in texture, about 2 minutes. Beat in the egg yolk and the almond extract. With a wooden spoon, beat in the flour and the almond sugar mixture.

3. Press the dough into a well-buttered 9-inch fluted tart pan with a removable bottom. With a fork, prick the bottom of the dough. Line the inside of the pastry-filled pan with aluminum foil and weight the dough with dry beans or rice. Bake for about 10 minutes, until the dough is set. Remove the foil and beans and continue baking until the pie shell is lightly browned, about 10 minutes longer. Cool the pie shell for 2 minutes.

4. Lightly beat the egg white with a fork and brush the inside of the baked shell with some of the egg white. Arrange the peach slices in concentric circles in the shell and pour any juices over them. Dot with the remaining 1 tablespoon of butter.

5. Place the tart in the oven and bake until the peaches are tender and the crust is golden brown, 30 to 40 minutes. Cool completely on wire rack before serving.

Lagniappes: Brushing the pie shell with egg white is another trick to discourage a soggy crust.

To peel peaches, drop them into boiling water for 1 minute. With a slotted spoon, transfer them to a bowl of cold water. Let stand 1 minute. Slip off the skins, cut in half lengthwise, and remove the pits.

Ste. Genevieve is the oldest permanent settlement in Missouri.

Banana Ice Cream with Praline Rum Sauce

⚓

Bananas Foster, bananas in a warm rum sauce served over ice cream, was invented by the kitchen of New Orleans's Brennan's restaurant in honor of a frequent patron. I couldn't resist taking the ingredients and mixing them up to make a scrumptious banana ice cream topped with a rich pecan-studded caramel sauce.

Makes 1 ¹/₂ quarts ice cream and 3 cups sauce, 6 to 8 servings

BANANA ICE CREAM
3 cups half-and-half
1 cup sugar
4 large egg yolks
4 medium ripe bananas, peeled
2 tablespoons lemon juice

CARAMEL RUM SAUCE
1 cup (2 sticks) unsalted butter

4 ounces (1 cup) coarsely chopped pecans or walnuts
2 cups packed light brown sugar
¾ cup heavy cream
4 tablespoons dark rum or an additional 2 tablespoons heavy cream

1. *Make the Ice Cream.* In a medium saucepan, bring the half-and-half and sugar to a simmer over low heat, stirring often to dissolve the sugar. Remove from the heat and let stand for 30 minutes.

2. In a medium bowl, whisk the egg yolks until lightly beaten. Gradually whisk in the warm half-and-half mixture. Rinse out the saucepan and return the mixture to it. Using a wooden spoon, stir the half-and-half mixture constantly over medium-low heat until thick enough to lightly coat the back of the spoon, 3 to 4 minutes. (An instant-read thermometer inserted into the mixture should read about 175°F.) Do not let the custard boil. Strain the mixture through a wire strainer into a medium bowl set into a larger bowl of ice water. Stirring often, let the custard cool until very cold, about 20 minutes.

3. In a blender or food processor fitted with a metal blade, purée the bananas with the lemon juice until very smooth. (You should have approximately 2 cups of purée.) Whisk the banana purée into the custard.

4. Freeze the custard in an ice-cream maker according to the manufacturer's instructions. Transfer the ice cream to an airtight container and freeze until firm, at least 4 hours, or overnight.

5. *Make the Sauce.* In a medium saucepan, melt 2 tablespoons of the butter over low heat. Add the pecans and cook, stirring often, until the pecans are lightly toasted and fragrant, about 2 minutes. Transfer to a bowl and set aside.

6. In the same saucepan, melt the remaining 14 tablespoons of butter. Stir in the brown sugar and cream and bring to a simmer, whisking often, until smooth. Off the heat, stir in the pecans and rum. Transfer to a sauceboat and let cool until lukewarm. (The sauce will thicken upon cooling.) Serve the ice cream with the warm sauce.

Lagniappe: Use well-ripened but not black-ripe bananas. The riper the bananas, the better the ice cream's flavor.

Persimmon Jumbles

⚓

These spice-scented cookies from my friend Judith's mother were made to be dunked in a glass of cold milk. Missourians would use tangerine-sized native American persimmons and black walnuts in the dough. American persimmons are easily found in Mississippi riverbank gardens but very difficult to find commercially. They are never picked until touched by frost, as the fruit is inedibly tannic but transformed into sweetness by the cold weather. Luckily, the Asian varieties (found at the greengrocers in autumn and early winter) work too. Choose the plump pear-shaped Hachiya variety, not the squat Fuyu persimmon, and be sure it is ripened to an exceedingly soft, almost translucent state. Flavorful black walnuts are more expensive than regular walnuts, mainly because their shells are incredibly hard and almost impossible to remove. Missourians have been known to use their car wheels as nutcrackers, running over the bags of nuts on the driveway.

Makes about 2 dozen cookies

2 medium well-ripened Hachiya persimmons, stems discarded (no need to peel)
2 cups all-purpose flour
1 teaspoon baking soda
½ teaspoon ground cinnamon
½ teaspoon ground allspice
½ teaspoon ground nutmeg
¼ teaspoon salt

8 tablespoons (1 stick) unsalted butter, at room temperature
1 cup sugar
1 large egg
1 cup chopped walnuts, preferably black walnuts
1 cup raisins

1. Preheat the oven to 375°F. Lightly butter two large cookie sheets. In a blender or food processor fitted with a metal blade, purée the persimmons until smooth. You should have 1 cup of purée. Sift the flour, baking soda, cinnamon, allspice, nutmeg, and salt together through a sieve onto a piece of waxed paper.

2. In a medium bowl, using an electric hand mixer on high speed, beat the butter and sugar until light in color and texture, about 2 minutes. Beat in the egg. Stir in the flour mixture to form a soft dough. Mix in the walnuts and raisins.

3. Drop the dough by scant tablespoons about 2 inches apart onto the prepared baking sheets. Bake until lightly browned, 12 to 15 minutes. Transfer the cookies to wire cake racks to cool completely. Store, tightly covered, at room temperature.

Lagniappes: Sweetened persimmon pulp (in the proportion of 1 cup pulp to 1 cup sugar) is available by mail order from Dymple's Delight, Route 4, P.O. Box 53, Mitchell, IN 47446 (812-849-3487).

Black walnuts are available from Missouri Dandy Pantry, 212 Hammonds Drive, Stockton, MO 65785 (1-800-872-6879).

Missouri produces more than 40 million pounds of black walnuts annually.

Suggested Reading

⚓

American Sternwheel Association, Inc. *Cruisin' Cuisine*. Collierville, TN: Fundcraft Publishing, 1988.

Brennan, Ella, and Dick Brennan. *The Commander's Palace New Orleans Cookbook*. New York: Clarkson N. Potter, Inc., 1984.

Brown, Dale. *The Cooking of Scandinavia*. New York: Time-Life Books, 1968.

Copage, Eric. *Kwanzaa: An African-American Celebration of Culture and Cooking*. New York: William Morrow and Company, Inc., 1991.

Engle, Allison, and Margaret Engel. *Food Finds*. Rev. ed. New York: Harper-Perennial, 1991.

Feibleman, Peter S. *American Cooking: Creole and Acadian*. New York: Time-Life Books, 1971.

Flexner, Marion W. *Out of Kentucky Kitchens*. 1949. Reprint. Lexington, KY: University Press of Kentucky, 1989.

Gandy, Joan W., and Thomas H. Gandy. *The Mississippi Steamboat Era in Historic Photographs*. New York: Dover Publications, Inc., 1987.

Hilliard, Sam Bowers. *Hog Meat and Hoecake: Food Supply in the Old South, 1840–1860*. Carbondale, IL: Southern Illinois University Press, 1972.

Lee, Hilde Gabriel. *Taste of the States: A Food History of America*. Charlottesville, VA: Howell Press, Inc., 1992.

Longstreet, Stephen, and Ethel Longstreet. *A Salute to American Cooking*. New York: Hawthorn Books, Inc., 1968.

Mariani, John. *The Dictionary of American Food and Drink*. 1st Ed. New Haven: Ticknor and Fields, 1983.

Middleton, Pat. *America's Great River Road*. Stoddard, WI: Heritage Press, 1991.

———. *America's Great River Road*. Vol. 2. Stoddard, WI: Heritage Press, 1992.

Samuel, Ray, Leonard V. Huber, and Warren C. Ogden. *Tales of the Mississippi*. New York: Hastings House Publishers, 1955.

Twain, Mark. *Life on the Mississippi*. New York: Penguin Books, 1984.

Wilson, Jose. *American Cooking: The Eastern Heartland*. New York: Time-Life Books, 1971.

Index

⚓